CURRENT AFRICAN ISSUES 49

I0027198

Water Scarcity and Food Security along the Nile

Politics, population increase and climate change

Terje Oestigaard

NORDISKA AFRIKAINSTITUTET, UPPSALA 2012

INDEXING TERMS:
River basins
Shared water resources
Water shortage
Food security
Population growth
Climate change
Geopolitics
International agreements
Regional development
Nile River

ISSN 0280-2171
ISBN 978-91-7106-722-7
© The author and Nordiska Afrikainstitutet 2012
Production: Byrå4
Print on demand, Lightning Source UK Ltd.

Contents

Foreword 5

Chapter 1 Introduction 7

Chapter 2 The global context: Water and food scarcity? 14

Chapter 3 The River Nile and the need for water... 25

Chapter 4 Agreements and disagreements 34

Chapter 5 Climate change, water systems and development.. 45

Chapter 6 Water and food production in the Nile Basin.. 55

Chapter 7 Virtual water, water wars and water riots... 68

Chapter 8 Future challenges and uncertainties – political implications?......................... 78

References 82

List of figures and tables

Figure 1 Map of the Nile Basin. Source: siteresources.worldbank.org 9

Table 1 Area of NBI member states and the area within the basin 27

Table 2 Population in the Nile Basin Countries (UN projections)..................................... 31

Table 3 Population in the Nile Basin Countries (US projections)...................................... 31

Table 4 Rural population, poverty headcount ratio at national poverty line and Gross
National Income per capita in Nile Basin countries 32

This *Current African Issues* is meant precisely as that: a discussion of a current African issue of utmost importance today and increasing importance in the future. However, writing about the Nile is a difficult task because of the very complexity of the subject. Not only does the Nile Basin cover approximately one-tenth of the African continent and the 11 countries have more than 400 inhabitants, the actors and factors influencing the development of the region are constantly changing and it is difficult if not impossible to be up-to-date and have a full overview of the situation. In a river system as complex as the Nile, there will also be very different and contradictory views and perceptions regarding the river, the actors and the issues. The premises are rapidly changing and much can happen even in the time it takes to publish this text after I have read the last draft. Added to this, there is a vast body of literature on the region and the river written from different perspectives and using various and sometimes incoherent empirical data and statistics.

Thus, on the one hand, there are many scholars with more knowledge than me on these issues who have written extensively about the Nile and the future challenges. As part of the *Current African Issues* series, this book is not primarily directed at this group of scholars and a readership well aware of the importance of the Nile today and in the future. On the other hand, despite the overall importance of water to all development and the Nile Basin in particular, many scholars, politicians and planners are still not fully aware of the fundamental role water plays and will play in society and development. Thus, there is an ever greater need to increase awareness of the role and importance of water.

Given both the complexity of the subject and current space limitations (as well as my own limitations), I pretend in no way to give a full description or analysis of the current situation in the Nile Basin. Rather, the aim is to present an overview of the complexity of the Nile and of the fundamental stakes involved today and onwards. Furthermore, the aim is to describe some of the greatest challenges, current and prospective, and to highlight different water theories addressing these topics.

I have tried to refer to the most up-to-date theories, empirical data and statistics, to present divergent opinions and data, and to write as objectively as possible, since different perspectives also have political implications. Any errors of fact or flawed interpretations are solely my own. However, I would like to thank Dr Anders Jägerskog, Prof. Terje Tvedt, Dr Tore Sætersdal of the Nile Basin Research Programme at the University of Bergen, Norway, and Prof. Kjell Havnevik for discussions and support, and the Nordic Africa Institute for providing a stimulating environment and workplace. I would also like to thank

Sonja Johansson for coordinating the practical aspects and Peter Colenbrander for commenting upon the language.

A note about the references. Quotations from politicians, newspaper articles and internet-pages are referred to in footnotes, otherwise references in the text have been used. Finally, the volume of water in the Nile is generally measured in 'bcm', billion cubic metres, and the Nile has an annual average of 84 bcm of water as measured at Aswan in Egypt, a measure that will be elaborated below.

Terje Oestigaard
Uppsala, June 2012

'The situation is rather desperate'

> *The conservation of water and the control of rivers for irrigation and hydroelectric*
> *power are of increasing importance in the world today. Growing populations and*
> *higher standards of living in areas which only a few years ago would have been called*
> *backward, are causing increasing demands on natural resources. The production of*
> *more food has become a matter of vital concern, not only to localised communities*
> *but to mankind as a whole. There are few places where these observations apply*
> *more acutely than the Nile valley ... Both [the White and Blue Nile] cross national*
> *frontiers and are a matter of wide concern, for wise compromise and goodwill must*
> *prevail if any system of control in the future is to benefit all those who have a natural*
> *right to a share in their waters.* Jonglei Investigation Team (1953:33)

This is not a description written today, but is a characterisation of the Nile situation almost 60 years ago by the Jonglei Investigation Team. Using Egypt as an example, the country has experienced increased water stress since the introduction of perennial cultivation during the era of Muhammad Ali in the first half of the 19th century. Between 1882 and 1900, Egypt's population increased from less than 7 million to about 10 million. The need for more water and a more secure water supply led to the building of the Aswan Dam between 1899 and 1902. It has been twice heightened, in 1912 and 1933. From 1900 to 1927, the population increased to more than 14 million (Langer 1936). Thus, wrote historian William L. Langer in 1936, 'the conversion of all available land has therefore become more and more imperative, but even so the situation is rather desperate' (Langer 1936:266). Egypt was still haunted by threats of floods and famines, and with the construction of the Aswan High Dam the hope was that these threats would be removed forever (Joesten 1960:62). Thus, the High Dam was part of Egypt's efforts to feed and improve the living standards of her people, because 'in Egypt, agricultural output simply could not keep pace with the population explosion, and the uncertainty of water supply was no longer tolerable' (Benedick 1979:120). Moreover, with the storage of water behind the dam on Egyptian soil, water exploitation was under Egyptian control, creating political stability and enabling hydropower (Benedick 1979:123).

Writing in 1979 on the impact and consequences of the High Dam, at a time when Egypt had a population of 39–40 million, Richard E. Benedick, who was coordinator of population affairs at the US Department of State, concluded that 'the seemingly inexorable population growth in recent years means that the long tradition of man-made works along the Nile will not end with the construction of the Aswan High Dam ... population growth has transformed what used to be overall food surplus into deficit: Egypt must now import a third of its food supply' (Benedick 1979:141–2). By the end of the 1970s, it was already expected that Egypt's population would reach about 70 million by the end of the century. It was also reckoned that the Aswan High Dam had bought only limited breathing space and that in future land and water would be limiting factors. 'A plausible future strategy for Egypt ... might be to abandon any hope of feeding itself, accept a growing dependence on foreign food sources, and concentrate development efforts on light manufactures and such high-value export crops as rice, cotton, fruits and vegetables', Benedick argued. 'It cannot be overemphasized, however, that limitation of population growth is the essential prerequisite for future economic and social betterment in Egypt' (Benedick 1979:144).

Thus, population increase and food security are intrinsically related to available water resources. Declining water reserves led Saudi Arabia to abandon its food self-sufficiency in 2007 and wheat production is planned to be phased out by 2016 (Anseeuw *et al.* 2012:37). Today, the Egyptian population is still increasing and the country imports more and more food to satisfy its needs and demands. With increasing population there is also increasing water stress, leading to water scarcity. Water scarcity is defined as 'the point at which the aggregate impact of all users impinges on the supply or quality of water under prevailing institutional arrangements to the extent that the demand by all sectors, including the environment, cannot be satisfied fully' (UN Water 2007:4).

There are some central themes in the history of the Nile Basin. First, water scarcity and water control along the Nile have been fundamental concerns, particularly in Egypt over the last two centuries, but also in other Nile Basin countries following independence. Development of water infrastructure, including food production systems, is fundamental to the welfare of any people. Second, continuous and ever increasing population growth is a major threat to water and food security, thus putting more pressure on limited water resources. This predicament is not unique to Egypt, and rapid and dramatic population growth in the whole Nile Basin will in coming decades increase the water stress of all living within the basin. Finally, with regard to current circumstances and future scenarios in the Nile Basin, the historical example of Egypt may point to a paradox between existing knowledge and political implementation. On one hand, as in Egypt, future water challenges are identified and made explicit long before they actually manifest themselves in scarcity. On the other, political solutions regarding water and food security are often implemented too late to satisfy current and future needs.

However, the problems associated with implementing policy to meet future water and food demands are not easy to solve. Much knowledge regarding these issues exists, but a lot of it is uncertain. On one hand, current data regarding today's challenges are often unreliable or inaccurate, making statistics more or less qualified guestimates. On the other, estimates about the future are by definition uncertain. Nevertheless, future predictions and scenarios are based on the best knowledge currently available and political implementation will also have to take these uncertainties into account. But how can one make the right political decisions without certain knowledge? Nonetheless, it is often on such a basis that political decisions are made and politicians are used to dealing with such uncertainties in the short run. The difficulty is that short-term solutions may not necessarily be the best in the longer run.

FIG. 1. MAP OF THE NILE BASIN[1]

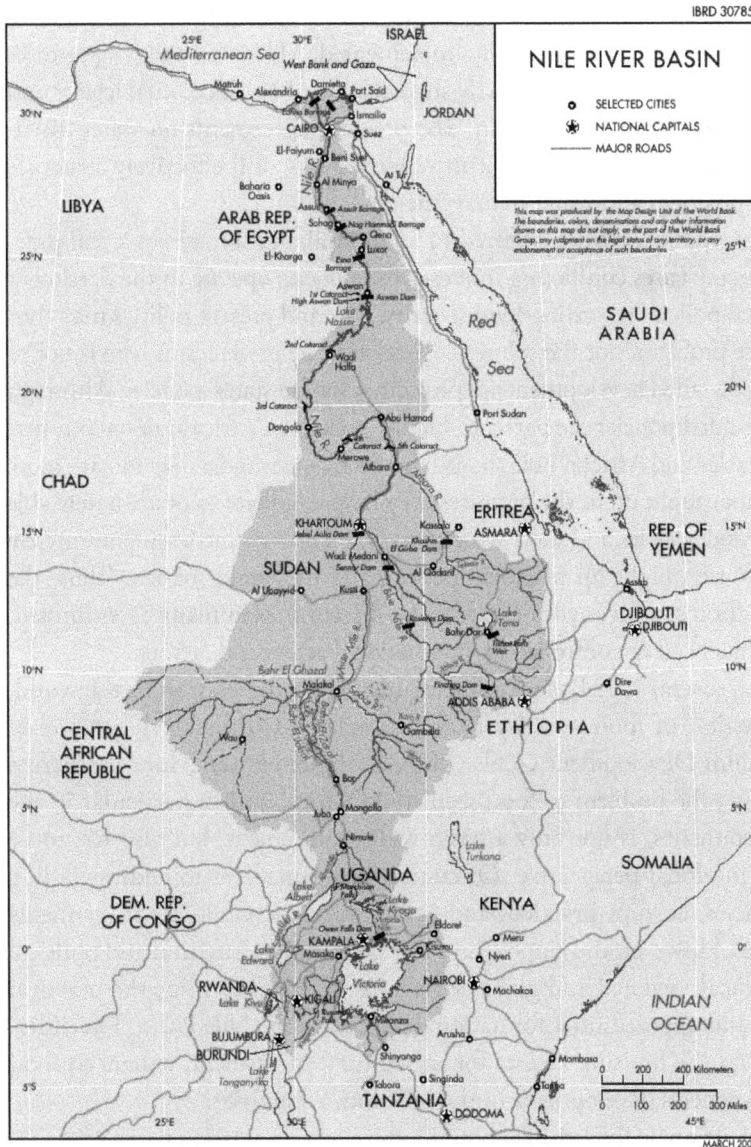

1. http://siteresources.worldbank.org/INTAFRNIL-BASINI/About%20Us/21082459/ Nile_River_Basin.htm.

Water and food

Thus, the aim of this publication is to highlight future challenges and uncertainties regarding water and water use in the Nile Basin. More precisely, the aim is to address and emphasise the important role of water and food security in decades to come. Although food security in general is seen as an obvious and major policy objective for individual nation states, in practice it seems that in many Nile Basin countries food security is not a primary concern. To corroborate this statement, it is necessary to analyse not only what politicians say, but also what crops are cultivated by what means and what kinds of agricultural projects are developed and politically implemented. Moreover, today's premises for agricultural development are partly shaped by the British colonial legacy and by Britain's vision for the Nile Basin. The previous agreements on water distribution and usage, as well as the British water systems, still effectively structure agricultural practices and water management.

'Good governance' is often referred to as an ideal and sometimes a real practice, but in many cases conflicting interests and policies operate to the detriment of agricultural policies regarding food security. Past and present politics may thus be part of the problem, not the solution. That said, the present aim here is not to criticise specific failed development aid projects or nation states' policies. Although current misguided policies are partly to blame, politics in Africa is not about performing miracles and African politicians have no magic wands: they too are more often than not caught up in the premises they have to adhere to or are barely able to change. Food policies and food security in Nile Basin countries are not merely national, but are caught up in global politics and the world market. Thus, the actual room for manoeuvre with regard to food security is in many cases limited, and often influenced or controlled by international actors and factors.

Moreover, several Nile Basin countries are among the poorest in the world, and the question of food security is also associated with achieving many of the Millennium Development Goals (MDGS) to turn poverty into prosperity. Hence, solving the problem of food security in Africa, and in particular in the Nile Basin countries, is not only a basin-wide requirement, but also has to be understood in global perspective. Of course, it is important to address failing African policies, corrupt practices and unsuccessful development investments and strategies. However, the emphasis in this book is the structural and political premises at local, regional and global scales that largely determine the practical possibilities and opportunities for national policies in the Nile Basin. Put differently, what are the limiting factors for agricultural investment, enhanced food security and general development in the Nile Basin countries?

The main rationale for writing about food security in relation to water is that food production is dependent on water: without water, there is no cultivation. Food production is the single biggest source of consumption of the globe's fresh water. Globally, about 70 per cent of the earth's fresh water is used for agricultural production. However, the globe's water resources are unevenly distributed and many areas with some of the highest rural and urban populations are located where there is limited water and consequently great water scarcity. The Nile Basin is identified as one hot spot where there will be increased water stress in the future. Within the basin, water resources are also unevenly distributed and some countries and regions have more water than others. Herein lies one of the fundamental challenges: upstream or riparian use of water affects downstream users, and how is it possible to share a basin's water in an equitable manner, when some regions have more water than others? Egypt is already one of the world's most water-scarce countries and is unable to produce enough food for its population. Increased population pressure and upstream agricultural development, mainly in irrigation projects but also different forms of rain-water harvesting, will affect the volume of water in the Nile reaching Sudan and Egypt and hence their food security. Both now and in the future, all countries in the Nile Basin depend and will depend, some more than others, on utilisation of the Nile for their development. Thus, this book will chiefly address one question:

Will there be enough water in the Nile Basin for food production so that the basin as a whole or individual countries will achieve food security in the future?

Addressing this question is, however, fraught with uncertainty, which will recur throughout the analysis. These uncertainties also complicate political processes and implementation. Still, we know enough to stress the importance of the food security issue. In the literature, the year 2050 often crops up in future scenarios and takes on Doomsday characteristics. Nevertheless, the 2050 predictions are useful for several reasons. First, this is the near future, only some 35 years ahead. Developing water system structures is a long-term proposition, and is time, energy and cost consuming. Consequently, if such projects are not already being implemented or will not be in the planning phase in the near future, there is a real risk that future policy implementation will again be too late or not well adapted to forthcoming challenges.

Second, although the core question above about water availability in relation to food security may initially seem somewhat deterministic, most farmers and people living in rural areas in the Nile Basin (besides Egypt and parts of Sudan) will most likely be dependent on rainfed agriculture and their own food production in the future, thereby drawing attention to overall water availability.

Third, although predictions regarding population increase vary, there is general consensus on one uniform trend: the population will increase, quite dramatically in many regions, particularly sub-Saharan Africa. With increased population, there will be more stress on water and food resources. Based on the predictions of the number of people in Nile Basin countries by 2050, the population will have increased tenfold since 1950.

Fourth, there are the impacts and consequences of climate change. Although the predictions about the impact of climate change on particular regions are uncertain, this uncertainty should ideally be factored into policy implementations. Climate change is mainly discussed in terms of increased global temperatures as a consequence of higher carbon emissions in the atmosphere, but the actual consequences of climate change will be experienced as changes in water systems. The predicted increase in extreme rainfall variability is generally expected to result in both more and increasingly unpredictable droughts and devastating floods. Importantly, within the Nile Basin the consequences of climate change will be different in different places: some localities may receive more (and perhaps more favourable) rains and others less water – but nobody knows for sure. Adding to this uncertainty is the fact that climate change models are not precise enough at local and regional levels regarding where and when more droughts or floods will occur or whether the intensity of annual rain patterns will change. However, what is certain is that if and when a region experiences these climate and water system changes, food security will be threatened unless countries have developed sufficient and adaptive water structures.

Combined, these factors and uncertainties challenge political strategies, practical policy implementation and notions of 'good governance'. Moreover, long-term food security may also be jeopardised by agricultural developments in favour of quick-growing and high value cash crops for the international marked instead of subsistence and food crops for local and national markets. This is, however, a complex issue. In the short term, it may be advantageous to grow high-value crops to generate an income (regardless of how small) and use the cash to import cheaper food from elsewhere (for poor farmers there is no cheap food, only a small gross margin between what is sold and bought). This may also increase a country's food security in the short run and at the same time stimulate the national economy, and many governments favour such policies, for instance Egypt and Ethiopia. And if you are a poor, hungry or starving farmer, why grow food? This question may seem counterintuitive. However, for an individual it may make more sense to grow valuable cash crops and buy cheaper food imports than to produce subsistence crops for own consumption. In the global world everyone needs money. Subsistence farming with no possibility of earning cash implies that farmers stay in poverty. Thus, for both governments and individual farmers there are many good reasons not to use agricultural land for food production in the short run. How this relates to food security in the long run is another question, which this book also aims to address.

The latter aspect links water and food scarcity and security in the Nile Basin to the world, global food production and the international market. If within a capitalist economy it is preferable to grow high cash-generating crops (whether food or not) for sale and import cheaper food from other places, who will produce this cheaper food and where? Today and in the predicted near future, more and more agricultural land will not be used for food production but for crops for industrial or other purposes. At the same time, the population in the Nile Basin and the world is increasing and there is an ever greater global need for food. In addition, today half the earth's population lives in cities and the percentage is expected to increase to 70 per cent by 2050. In other words, more than two-thirds of the world's population will need food they have not produced themselves. With an agricultural system governed by the international market, several questions arise. Will there be enough water for food production both globally and in the Nile Basin? Where will what types of food be produced? Can all be winners in this world system? How will the international market affect the agricultural economies and food security priorities of sub-Saharan countries, today among the poorest in the world? To address these questions it is necessary to start with current and future scenarios regarding global water and food scarcity before examining the Nile Basin.

Is there enough water and food in the world today and will there be in the future?

The short answer to these two questions is yes, but the real question is how relevant this observation is. In the world, the amount of fresh water is constant and with population growth the demand for fresh water is increasing. Still, on a global scale there is and will be enough land, water and human resources to produce sufficient food throughout the next 50 years (Molden *et al.* 2007:61–2).

Today there are 7 billion people on earth, a number that is expected to reach beyond 9 billion in 2050. In 1800, the number was one billion and in 1950 2.5 billion. According to UN estimates, almost all of this population growth up to 2050 will be in developing countries (UN 2009). Of the 9.2 billion people, it is estimated that about 86 per cent will live in less developed countries and, as already noted, about 70 per cent in rapidly growing urban areas (Rosegrant *et al.* 2009:206). After 2050, the global population is expected to level off, except in sub-Saharan Africa (Molden *et al.* 2007:77). With this increased population in developing countries and in sub-Saharan Africa, will there be enough food and water for food production in regions with the highest population increase and density?

Thomas Malthus's thesis more than two centuries ago was that the world's natural resources could not expand to produce enough food for the growing population. 'The power of population is so superior to the power of the earth to produce subsistence for many that premature death must in some shape or another visit the human race' (Malthus 1798). In other words, with increased population growth there would not be enough food. His interpretation has been heavily criticised from all directions, and Boserup (1965) inverted the argument by arguing that increased population is one of the major drivers of increased food production and agricultural development.

On a global scale, Malthus's argument has been wrong or at least partly incorrect, but it still has relevance for sub-Saharan Africa (Bohle 2001:5729) and thus for certain of the Nile Basin countries. Therefore, following Malthus, how relevant is it if there is enough food worldwide but Africa starves while the US and Europe throw away enormous amounts of food? Asia has undergone a 'Green Revolution', but why has this not happened in Africa? Why does Malthus's thesis still have particular relevance to sub-Saharan Africa, but not necessarily elsewhere? Again, this puts the emphasis on political and structural premises both within and beyond the Nile Basin countries.

It is estimated that there will be a demand for 40 per cent more water for farming, industrial and urban needs in Africa by 2030 (UNECA ACPC 2011:3). From 2010 to 2100, the overall population increase in the world is expected to be about 3 billion, of which Africa will account for about 2.5 billion people.[2] Thus, 'there is no development without water, but there is not enough water for development'.[3] Malthus may have been wrong in 1798, but as long as there is hunger one cannot outright dismiss his thoughts. Moreover, with Africa's population increasing at an unprecedented rate, 'history is no longer a reliable means of predicting future water demand and availability' (UN Water 2012:18). This will be an immense challenge for a continent that already has the highest poverty rates. 'Global food security is a major challenge for public policies. In fact, the reduction of poverty and hunger is the first MDG. The state of natural resources, especially water, is becoming an increasingly limiting factor in dealing with this challenge' (CGAAER 2012:15).

Although food may be abundant on the world market, a poor household's ability to secure food through markets and non-market possibilities may be limited or decline. The main question for food security and agricultural economies is thus whether food systems can keep pace with the growing demand during times of climate change and population increase (Vermeulen *et al.* 2012:137).

The reason population increase cannot be overstressed as *the* main challenge to development, poverty eradication and food security on a global scale but particularly in the Nile Basin is simple, and somehow in direct continuation of Malthus's line of thought: will there be enough water and food for all the people? As is commonly pointed out, on a global scale there is enough water: the main problem is management (Human Development Report 2006:133). Nevertheless, the global average is largely irrelevant because at one level the world's water is like the world's wealth: 'globally, there is more than enough to go around: the problem is that some countries get a lot more than others' (Human Development Report 2006:135). This has also been taken as an argument in favour of rejecting Malthus' hypothesis, since good management and policies could enable food surpluses in areas where there are water and food shortages. In practice, this means reducing water waste and not cultivating water-intensive crops such as cotton and rice in arid regions (Human Development Report 2006:141). But water management practices are not separate from policies and there are no value-free or objective water contexts. If water management policies or their absence define or are part of the problem, then the outcome may be food shortages, famine and ultimately death: there is not enough water or food production for the population (given the social organisation associated with these resources).

Today, several Nile Basin countries rank among the poorest in the world.

2. Alexander Müller, assistant director-general natural resources management and environment department, FAO, World Water Forum, Marseilles, 13 March 2012.
3. http://www.worldwaterforum6.org/en/news/single/article/blue-gold-for-green-growth/ (accessed 19 March 2012).

At the same time, many of the same countries are rich in resources, underscoring the point that poverty is not only a matter of absence of resources at local or national level, but also of uneven distribution and failed policies. With this political dimension of poverty in mind, one may rephrase the question: why do you need water and food within a country's national borders?

By any standard, Singapore is perhaps one of the wonders of the world when it comes to development. The nation is essentially a city-state with a population of about 5 million. Apart from the main island, the country comprises of 62 other islands, and covers a total area of of only 710 square kilometres. Today, Singapore boasts one of the world's booming economies and it is one of the most advanced cities in the world. Less than 40 years ago, the city was a slum. Singapore has hardly any natural water resources, and agriculture contributes nothing to the national economy. Water comes from Malaysia and food from elsewhere in the world. Everything is imported because the country has one of the fastest expanding economies globally (the concept of virtual water and its relevance will be discussed in Chapter 7). Nationally, it is thus possible to develop a country even if it has no natural resources.

Although Singapore is a country and a nation, from a water perspective it is first and foremost a city. Today, more than 50 per cent of the world's population lives in urban areas, a number that will continue to grow. Thus, there is an ever increasing need for more food production to feed the urban population. However, the example of Singapore may be misleading in terms of how it is possible to develop a country needing imports of food and 'virtual water', but it does exemplify to the phenomenon of increased urbanism. The urban population needs food, which has to be produced in rural areas. Cities (and a country) like Singapore cannot be developed and sustained without the production of surplus agricultural products.

On paper and in practice, it is possible with good governance to develop a poor country and sustain a high population within a limited geographical area without natural resources. Thus, contrary to Malthus, it is perfectly possible to develop a country far beyond its national water and food endowments, but this exacts a price at local, national and global levels. In a global world, not all countries can import all their water and food. Food has to be produced somewhere, and agriculture needs water. Globally, the market economy may enable some countries to import all their water and food, but this will not and cannot be the solution for the majority of the earth's population. Moreover, one consequence of Singapore's development is that it lacks all national food self-sufficiency. In practice, Singapore has no option because of the lack of water resources and limited areas of land available for agriculture. Saudi Arabia was forced to abandon its food self sufficiency in 2007 because of declining water reserves. In the future, Nile Basin countries may also be forced to abandon their policies of food self-sufficiency because of lack of water. If this happens, it will in practice be a consequence of decreasing water resources in combination with increasing population. At an overall level, however, is this a preferable policy and development path?

Poverty and food production

Today, global agriculture accounts for about 70 per cent of all water use, but up to 95 per cent in several developing countries (UN Water 2007:21). In rural Africa, about 80–90 per cent of the population relies upon producing and eating its own food (UN Water 2007:13).

The UN slogan 'We can end poverty,' the main MDG aim, to be achieved by 2015, looks good on paper and has achieved results in eradicating extreme poverty in some places. The most successful poverty alleviation has happened in China and India (but importantly, the economic development in China has taken place independently of UN's Millennium Goals). By contrast, sub-Saharan Africa is still falling behind. Despite significant reductions in extreme poverty, the proportions of people going hungry remained stable, partly as a result of the current economic crises and increasing food prices. In particular, sub-Saharan Africa will be unable to reach the hunger reduction target by 2015 (Millennium Development Goals Report 2011).

Behind the political visions and statistics are real people. Even if the proportion of hungry people has remained constant, with increased population the actual number has grown in sub-Saharan Africa and the food insecurity situation has thus worsened. About 60 per cent of those facing food insecurity live in South Asia and sub-Saharan Africa (Wani *et al.* 2009:1). From 1980 to 2000, the number of the food insecure almost doubled from 125 million to 200 million (Fraiture, Molden and Wichelens 2010:497). In the period 1992–2002, the absolute number of undernourished Africans increased by about 20 per cent and in the world today more than one billion people live in food-insecure situations (Matondi, Havnevik and Beyene 2011:10).

To meet the MDGs, it is necessary to improve water management and invest in water for food. In 2007, the UN (UNDP 2007) concluded that it is not a lack of arable land that will be the major constraint in coming decades, but water scarcity. The main factors that will affect food production are the: 1) water (and in some areas, land) crisis, 2) climate change crisis, 3) energy prices, and 4) credit crisis (Hanjra and Quereshi 2010:366–7).

Globally, about 12 per cent of the total land area is used for agricultural production and about 42 per cent of the world's population live on this land (Fraiture *et al.* 2009:124). Only 19 per cent of cultivated land on the globe is irrigated, but this land produces 40 per cent of the world's food (Hanjra and Quereshi 2010:365). By 2050, it is expected that food demand will increase by

70–90 per cent (Fraiture *et al.* 2009:124) and that global cereal demand will be between 2,800 and 3,200 million tons, an increase of 55–80 per cent on today. Projections for meat demand range between 375 and 570 million tons, an increase of 70–155 per cent (Fraiture, Molden and Wichelens 2010:496). With global population increase, agricultural water use has grown substantially and will continue to do so not only because there will be more mouths to feed, but also because people are richer, consume more water and demand products such as meat, fish, dairy and sugar. Today, it is estimated that the total use of water for crop cultivation lies between 6,800 and 7,500 km³, and the Comprehensive Assessment estimate is 7,130 km³. This amount of water represents an average of about 3,000 litres per person per day for all of the world's people (Fraiture and Wichelns 2010:503). It is expected that crop water consumption will increase by 70–90 per cent by 2050, depending on population increase and income distribution, thus ranging between 12,050 to 13,500 km³ (Fraiture and Wichelens 2007:99).

Different studies come up with different estimates and predictions, but there is general consensus regarding water use in agriculture in the present and future. In one study, the lower estimate of about 6,800 km³/year of water to produce the globe's food today was used. In order to feed the earth's population in 2050 (on 3,000 cal per person per day), the total agricultural water consumption was estimated at about 12,400 km³/year. Based on this analysis, an additional 5,600 km³/year will be required, of which only 800 km³/year will be blue/irrigation water. The remaining 4,800 km³ will have to come from new green (rain) water resources. However, since the amount of precipitation is constant, achieving this surplus from existing precipitation will have to be achieved through horizontal expansion or by converting evaporation into transpiration. Estimates suggest it will be possible to improve rainfed areas and thus enable another 1,500 km³/year of water. However, there would still be a shortfall of 3,300 km³/year in the water needed to meet the world's food production. Consequently, if this shortfall is not addressed, there will be a food gap that will affect global food security and will mainly prevail in South Asia and sub-Saharan Africa (Hanjra and Quereshi 2010:369–70).

Other studies, however, argue that African food production is a largely untapped resource with vast possibilities (Juma 2011). Moreover, if water for agriculture is managed better, there will be enough land and resources to produce food for the next 50 years (Fraiture and Wichelns 2010:502). Given the predicted increase in food production of about 70 per cent by 2050, it is expected that most of this increase will have to come from intensification of food systems and about 15 per cent from expansion of agricultural areas (Cook *et al.* 2011:1).

In short, on paper there will be enough water for food production in the decades to come, which in theory will be sufficient to feed the world's increasing population. This depends on good governance and management of water and food resources, and this is where the main challenges to food security in the Nile Basin lie.

Food security, risks and vulnerability

'Water is a natural resource upon which all social and economic activities and ecosystem functions depend' (UN Water 2012:23). Food security is defined as the point at which 'all people, at all times, have physical and economic access to sufficient, safe and nutritious food to meet their dietary needs and food preferences for an active and healthy life' (FAO 1996), and as 'a necessary if not sufficient basis for poverty alleviation' (Cook *et al.* 2011:2). According to the World Food Council:

> Food security implies two things. First, ... that food is available, accessible, affordable – when and where needed – in sufficient quantity and quality. Second, it implies an assurance that this state of affairs can reasonably be expected to continue ... that it can be sustained. To put it simply, food security exists when adequate food is available to all people on a regular basis. (World Food Council 1988:2)

By contrast:

> Chronic food insecurity is a continuously inadequate diet caused by the inability to acquire food. It affects households that persistently lack the ability either to buy food or produce their own. Transitory food insecurity is a temporary decline in a household's access to enough food. It results from instability in food prices, food production, or household incomes – and in its worst form it produces famine. (World Bank 1986:1)

Thus, global food prices can be linked to climate change and the vulnerability of rainfed agriculture, where the successful harvest depends on the arrival of seasonal rains at the right time and in sufficient amount.

One may differ on or identify different types of droughts from an analytical perspective, although all of them are characterised by insufficient water or water at the wrong time for agricultural purposes. First, there is unpredictable drought, which occurs when total precipitation is comparable to normal years, but the harvest is exposed to growth stress as a result of unpredictable, erratic and uneven rainfall. Second, there is full-season drought, which occurs when overall precipitation patterns are much lower than in normal years and plants do not receive enough water. Third, there is terminal drought, which occurs when initially there is enough water for cultivation, but later the soil is exposed to a water deficit. Fourth, there is intermittent drought, which occurs when there is a short dry spell during the growing season and the harvest is exposed to drought only at one stage during growth (UNECA ACPC 2011:19).

Variability in rainfall generates dry spells almost every season and hence shorter periods of water stress during the growing season. Dry spells are manageable and investments in water infrastructure can overcome these fluctuations, which may last from two to four weeks. Meteorological droughts, on the other hand, occurring on average once a decade in moist semi-arid regions and up to twice per decade in dry semi-arid regions, result in complete crop failure. When such droughts occur, they cannot be counteracted by agricultural water management, and other social coping strategies are necessary, such as food relief and grain banks (Wani *et al.* 2009:8). When the rain and the harvest fail, farmers have to buy their food for survival on the global market, where prices increase and fluctuate during periods of drought.

Currently, food prices are extremely volatile, although in general food prices have decreased in absolute and relative terms over the past two decades. Nevertheless, food prices have increased sharply in recent years, mainly due to the increased production of agricultural products for non-food use (Fraiture, Molden and Wichelens 2010:495). During 2007 and 2008, food prices increased rapidly worldwide. The price of wheat and maize doubled between 2003 and 2008. A major reason for this increase is the demand for biofuel and it is estimated that between 2000 and 2007 agricultural production of biofuels contributed to an average global increase in cereal prices of approximately 30 per cent. Although food prices have decreased since mid-2008, in 2009 they were still 30–50 per cent higher on average than a decade earlier (Havnevik 2011:21–2). In March 2011, the food price index was 36 per cent higher than in 2010 and remained close to the 2008 peak (Food Price Watch 2011a). Between June 2010 and June 2011, prices in Ethiopia, for instance, increased by 86 per cent for wheat and 64 per cent for maize (Food Price Watch 2011b). Importantly, there are huge differences, fluctuations and increases in African domestic food prices even when global food prices decline or remain unchanged (Food Price Watch 2011c).

The previous stability in world food supply and generally declining prices were mainly due to irrigation, but this has had not only financial costs. Many irrigation systems have failed or resulted in environmental degradation and reduced water flows into wetlands (Faurès *et al.* 2007:355). Nevertheless, 'irrigation will remain critical in supplying cheap, high-quality food, and its share of world food production will rise to more than 45 per cent by 2030, from 40 per cent today' (Faurès *et al.* 2007:354).

In sub-Saharan Africa, poverty rates in general are lower for farmers in irrigated farming than in rainfed and other agricultural systems (Castillo and Namara *et al.* 2007:154). More than 95 per cent of the land used for farming in sub-Saharan Africa is rainfed, and globally most countries depend on rainfed agriculture as their subsistence basis. In sub-Saharan Africa, agriculture accounts for 35 per cent of GDP and employs about 70 per cent of the population.

Agriculture is thus key for economic development and poverty reduction, and every 1 per cent increase in agricultural production reduces the numbers of the absolute poor by 0.6–1.2 per cent (Wani *et al.* 2009:1–2).

Agricultural land for irrigation is, nevertheless, limited worldwide. Despite increases in irrigated agriculture, most of the world's agricultural production will come from rainfed agriculture (Molden *et al.* 2007:71). Rainfed agriculture will therefore also produce the bulk of the world's food in the future. Eighty per cent of the world's agricultural land is rainfed and produces 62 per cent of the world's staple foods. However, water productivity is in general very low and the challenge is to improve agricultural systems so that they can produce more with less fresh water (Rockström *et al.* 2007:317). In the coming 50 years, food demands in sub-Saharan Africa will roughly triple and irrigation is expected to meet only 7–11 per cent of total food production. Consequently, 'without substantial improvements in the productivity of rainfed agriculture, food production will fall short of demand' (Fraiture and Wichelens 2007:132).

In arid regions, absolute water scarcity is a major obstacle to agriculture whereas in semi-arid and dry sub-humid tropical regions seasonal rainfall is generally sufficient for successful harvests (Wani *et al.* 2009:7). Thus, according to Rockström, 'the key challenge is to reduce water-related risks posed by high rainfall variability rather than coping with an absolute lack of water' (Rockström *et al.* 2007:316). From this perspective, risks can thus be treated as 'exogenous', in the sense that they are not directly under the control of humans (Dercon 2005:484), and risk can be defined as 'a cause of poverty and its persistence' (Dercon 2005:485) directly related to water, food production and food security. 'Vulnerable households' can be defined as 'those liable to fall under an agreed poverty line over time and with a particularly high probability' (Dercon 2002:16) or as those for whom 'the existence and the extent of a *threat* of poverty and destitution' may result in 'a socially unacceptable level of well-being' (Dercon 2005:486).

However, from a water-perspective, risks cannot be solely reduced to a matter of rainfall variability. Whereas the vulnerability of households may be in accordance with an agreed poverty line, risks are not always 'exogenous'. With regard to water and the Nile, it is precisely the modification of water systems that allows even areas with an absolute lack of water to be cultivated, as the irrigation projects in Egyptian deserts testify. The risks associated with the absence of rain are controlled and directly under human control, as will be further elaborated in the discussion of the Aswan High Dam.

Poverty, hunger and water stress are intrinsically linked. Regions with rainfed agriculture often face challenges associated with water scarcity, fragile environments, drought and land degradation, high population pressure and low efficiency with regard to rainwater and investment in water infrastructure (Wani *et al.* 2009:5). Consequently, exposure to risk and risk-related vulnerability implies that people take precautions and that the responses to these risks have welfare consequences and implications for practices and policy (Dercon 2005:486). Analytically, one may therefore distinguish between risk-management strategies and risk-coping strategies. The first aims to reduce the risks before the shocks and suffering occur through, for instance, income diversification, farm and off-farm activities and seasonal migration. The latter deals with how the consequences of risks are handled after they occur, which may involve self-insurance or group-based risk-sharing within and between families and groups (Dercon 2002:4).

Importantly for agricultural development and policy implementation, there are different factors and actors. From a water systems perspective (Tvedt 2010a, 2010b) people and farmers have to adapt to physical waterscapes. This also involves modifying the water-world by procuring and securing more water at the right time, such as by developing irrigation schemes and advanced rain-harvesting techniques. Cultural and ideological aspects also structure the water-world with regard to agricultural production on the global market, creating possibilities and limitations.

Importantly, though, strategies that reduce risks and vulnerability for some, may increase insecurity for others. Fraiture and Wichelens pinpoint the dilemma eloquently:

> With increasing globalization, many poor farmers are affected by developments in international markets. Thus, productivity investments alone might not be sufficient to ensure household food security if market prices decline when aggregate productivity increases. The challenge is to increase food production while not depressing prices below that level that enables farmers to earn sufficient revenue to achieve food security. Improving productivity at a pace that exceeds the rate of decline in market prices requires broader access to water. At the same time, the urban poor and the landless rural benefit from lower food prices. The landless rural poor also benefit from labor opportunities provided by large-scale irrigation development (Fraiture and Wichelens 2007:130–1).

The means to mitigate poverty for some may also increase poverty among others in a community, nation or watershed. At the centre of the question of food security is the use and utilisation of water resources and how agricultural products are part of the global world market. With an increasing population, there will be greater pressure on this vital and life-giving resource for all.

Water scarcity

In the literature, specific terminologies are used to refer to various aspects of the subject. 'Water use' refers to 'water that is being put to beneficial use by humans'. 'Water withdrawal' refers to the 'gross amount of water extracted from any source in the natural environment for human purposes'. 'Water demand' represents the 'volume of water needed for a given activity. If supply is unconstrained, water demand is equal to water withdrawal' (UN Water 2009:98).

Water scarcity is defined 'from the perspective of individual water users who lack secure access to safe and affordable water to consistently satisfy their need for food production, drinking, washing, or livelihoods' (Molden *et al.* 2007:57). Water scarcity is first and foremost a poverty issue. About 1.2 billion people live in areas of physical water scarcity and up to one in three people in the world face water shortages. In 2025, about 1.8 billion people will live in regions with absolute water scarcity and about two-thirds of the world's population in areas of water stress (UN Water 2007:4, 10). Importantly, 'the appropriate scale for understanding water scarcity is at the local or regional level, notably within a river basin or a sub-basin, rather than at the national or global level' (UN Water 2007:6). The basic metabolism of the human body requires about 1,800–2,000 kcal every day, with every calorie of food consuming about one litre of water in food production. Thus, producing enough food to satisfy a person's daily diet requires 2–3,000 litres of water. Only 2–3 litres of water are needed for drinking each day and between 20–300 litres for domestic needs (UN Water 2007:9). The greatest water consumer is therefore agriculture and the food we eat.

The Falkenmark indicator is commonly used to measure water stress. 'Water stress' is defined as an annual water supply below 1,700 cubic metres per person. 'Water scarcity' exists when annual water supply is below 1,000 cubic metres per person and 'absolute scarcity' when it is below 500 cubic metres per person (Falkenmark 1989). This indicator highlights the total run-off available for human use and distinguishes between climate and human-induced water scarcity. Subsequently, there have been other indices that have included different social variables, with the UNDP Human Development Index being widely accepted (Brown and Matlock 2011).

Regarding water footprint, 'a country's water footprint is the volume of water used in the production of all the goods and services consumed by inhabitants of the country'. In 2009, the global water footprint was 1,240 cubic metres per capita per year and there were huge differences between countries. The average water footprint in the US was 2,480 cubic metres per capita, whereas in China

it was 700 cubic metres (UN Water 2009:101). The relevance of the per capita
water footprint may, however, be limited and misleading because it says nothing about the relationship between actual water use and water availability. Put
differently, what is the relationship between possible water use and actual availability in time and space. Moreover, national averages conceal major differences
between rich and poor.

In any event, water stress indicators are precisely that: indicators. According to the World Bank, in Egypt the annual per capita share of fresh water is
less than 700 cubic metres/year and with predicted population growth the per
capita share is expected to fall to less than 300 cubic metres/year in 2050.[4] The
per capita share may even drop to 350 cubic metres by 2025.[5] Given that about
98 per cent of Egypt's fresh water comes from the Nile, such indications and
predictions may have higher accuracy than in regions with more diverse but un-
derused water resources. The UN estimates that annual water demand in Egypt
in 2050 will be more than 100 bcm (UN Water 2009:101), whereas the annual
average amount of water as measured at Aswan is 84 bcm.

Several water stress indexes rank Egypt as a country with extreme water
stress. According to one index, in 2011 Egypt was ranked number four[6] among
the world's most water-scarce countries and the World Bank ranked Egypt along
with Kuwait, United Arab Emirates, Libya and Saudi Arabia as the top five
countries at highest risk of water stress.[7] Other indexes place Egypt just beyond
the world's 'top-ten' water-stressed countries. The absolute ranking is irrelevant
and perhaps impossible to measure. The point is that Egypt is already a highly water-stressed country and will in the near future experience and face even
greater water stress. Moreover, in sub-Saharan Africa, the number of people
living in water-stressed countries is expected to rise from 30 per cent to 80 per
cent in 2025. All told, the water stress of all Nile Basin countries is expected to
increase, in many cases dramatically.

4. http://www-wds.worldbank.org/external/default/WDSContentServer/WDSP/MNA/20
11/12/15/622B9D22AD5B2B7A85257967003D11D9/1_0/Rendered/PDF/P1180900PI-
D0Ap015201101323947221905.pdf (accessed 29 February 2012).

5. A.H. Abd el Hadi, Country Report on Egyptian Agriculture, IPI regional workshop on
potassium and fertigation development in West Asia and North Africa, Rabat, Morocco,
24–28 November 2004 at http://www.ipipotash.org/udocs/Country per cent20Report per
cent20on per cent20Egyptian per cent20Agriculture.pdf (accessed 29 February 2012).

6. http://maplecroft.com/about/news/water_security.html (accessed 29 February 2012).

7. http://water.worldbank.org/water/news/middle-east-and-north-african-countries-highest-
risk-water-stress (accessed 29 February 2012.

A scarce resource

The River Nile is considered by many the most important river in the world. At 6,671km (there are different estimates), it is also the world's longest river. The Nile Basin catchment area spans 11 countries: Burundi, the Democratic Republic of Congo (DRC), Egypt, Eritrea, Ethiopia, Kenya, Rwanda, South Sudan, Sudan, Tanzania and Uganda. It drains an area of approximately 3,349,000 square kilometres, about one tenth of the African continent.

According to the Nile Basin Initiative (2012), in 2010 the total population in the basin countries was 424 million, of which 232 million lived in the basin (about 54 per cent). It is estimated that by 2025 some 600 million people will be living in the Nile Basin countries and more than 300 million in the basin. The utilisation of the Nile's waters has in recent history been a controversial issue. Water is already scarce in some parts of the basin and the future distribution of the Nile's waters will have global political consequences and will be fundamental to the development processes of the respective countries. Thus, 'regarded in a long-term historical and ecological perspective, the Nile should most fruitfully be seen as an a priori existing, supra-individual and changing order which in various ways and to different degrees has framed human action and development efforts in the basin' (Tvedt 2004:6).

All basin states are dependent on the Nile for their development, but in differing degree. With the expected population growth and the need for more water together with predicted climate change and possible reduction in the overall amount of water, each country will depend more on the Nile for its development and each drop of water will become more precious. 'The complex unity of a basin hydrology implies that diversions, abstractions or interferences with the flow of a river regime at any point in a basin eventually affect, albeit in varying scales, the quality and volume of water received by the head channels of river courses crossing international borders' (Kassa 2010:472). Moreover, global climate change means there are a lot of uncertainties regarding the Nile's water flow – will there be more or less water in the Nile, and which areas will experience more droughts and rain failures, and which more floods and heavier rains? Some predictions suggest there will be less water overall and that the Nile Basin will become drier, thus experiencing higher water stress. Consequently, if the waters of the Nile become even scarcer, will there be enough water for all? If not, will the Nile become a source of future conflict or cooperation?

The 1929 and 1959 Agreements

The waters of the Nile originate in both the White Nile and Blue Nile, which converge at Khartoum in Sudan to form the River Nile. The White Nile flows from Lake Victoria (and the other equatorial great lakes) and accounts for approximately 15 per cent of the Nile's waters, whereas the Ethiopian tributaries (the Blue Nile, Atbara and Sobat) contribute approximately 85 per cent of the Nile's waters as measured at Aswan in Egypt, where, as noted above, annual average total water is 84 bcm. However, although the river drains a catchment spread across 11 countries, past agreements have restricted the use and utilisation of the Nile waters to Egypt and Sudan.

In 1929, Egypt and Britain (on behalf of the East African colonies) negotiated the Nile Water Agreement, which stated that 'no irrigation or power works or measures are to be constructed or taken on the River Nile and its branches, or on the lakes from which it flows … in such a manner as to entail any prejudice to the interests of Egypt, either reduce the quantity of water arriving in Egypt, or modify the date of its arrival, or lower its level'.

In 1959, Egypt and Sudan signed an agreement *For the Full Utilisation of the Nile Waters,* dividing the totality of the Nile waters between themselves without inviting upstream countries to the negotiations. According to this agreement, of the Nile's annual average of 84 bcm, Egypt would receive 55.5 bcm and Sudan 18.5 bcm. The remaining 10 bcm were expected to be lost to evaporation, mainly from Lake Nasser. However, as with much of the data and statistics regarding the Nile, there are uncertainties, because it is also acknowledged that a minimum of about of 10 bcm need to flow out into the Mediterranean to preserve the ecosystems.

The 1959 agreement has been disputed by other Nile Basin states for a number of reasons. First, the agreement predates the independence of several of the countries, and to what extent is such an agreement still valid today? With regard to Ethiopia in particular, which was independent when the agreement was signed, is an agreement made by two countries binding on other countries excluded from the negotiations? Moreover, can downstream countries prevent upstream countries from using the water flowing through their territories? Contrariwise, can upstream countries deny downstream countries the use of the Nile, on which Egypt in particular is fundamentally dependent? Finally, can alternative water resources be developed and utilised in upstream countries, thereby enabling more Nile water to flow to downstream countries. If so, will downstream countries contribute financially to such development on the grounds that they will benefit from it?

In 1999 the Nile Basin Initiative (NBI) was established among the then 10 Nile countries (South Sudan became independent on 9 July 2011), with Eritrea having observer status. The aim of the Initiative was the negotiation of a new agreement that would include upstream countries. This agreement is the Cooperative Framework Agreement, which was signed in 2010 by five of the riparian countries (Ethiopia, Tanzania,Uganda, Rwanda and Kenya), with Burundi following suit in 2011. The Cooperative Framework Agreement is an international treaty laying down principles of cooperative water resource management among all the countries sharing the River Nile. Egypt and Sudan have strongly opposed the agreement, as will be seen in the next chapter, and this relates directly to the different interests in and needs for the Nile waters.

Different interests and needs

In the Nile Basin, there is a great difference between the sizes of the countries and the respective areas lying within the basin, with implications for the degree of dependence of the countries on Nile Basin water resources.

TABLE 1. AREA OF NBI MEMBER STATES AND THE AREA WITHIN THE BASIN

Burundi	Total area	28,702
	Area within basin	13,860
DR Congo	Total area	2,516,395
	Area within basin	21,796
Egypt	Total area	1,014,742
	Area within basin	302,452
Ethiopia	Total area	1,129,065
	Area within basin	365,318
Kenya	Total area	589,070
	Area within basin	51,363
Rwanda	Total area	25,107
	Area within basin	20,625
Sudan (includes South Sudan)	Total area	2,551,341
	Area within basin	2,062,558
Tanzania	Total area	937,762
	Area within basin	118,507
Uganda	Total area	244,491
	Area within basin	240,067

Source: Nile Basin Initiative 2012. The land mass in South Sudan is estimated to be approx. 640,000 square kilometres and the population between 7.5 and 9.7 million. The population is expected to increase by approximately 3 million over the coming six years as a result of natural growth and the return of refugees and displaced people (Granit et al. 2010:32).

Egypt is a downstream state where the Nile is literally the lifegiving artery of the country. Since time immemorial, the Nile has had a mystical and grand aura. The saying 'Egypt is the gift of the Nile' is attributed to Herodotus, but most likely it originates with Hecataeus of Miletus, who travelled through Egypt almost a century before Herodotus (Darby, Ghalioungui and Grivetti 1977:32). According to the philosophers of antiquity, the Nile was the most spectacular river in the world: 'The Nile surpasses all the rivers of the inhabited world in the benefactions to humanity', proclaimed Diodorus. Seneca, on the other hand, said that all rivers were 'vulgares aqua', but the Nile was the 'most noble' of all watercourses. Arnobius described the Nile as 'the greatest of rivers' and according to Ammianus Marcellinus it was 'a river which is kindly to all' (Wild 1981:88). The Egyptian writer Jamal Himdan expressed it this way: 'The first civilization was the fruit of fortunate geographical marriage between Egypt and the Nile, hence if history was a father of Egyptians and Egypt was a Mother of the World the Nile is simply the great, great grandfather of human civilization' (Himdan 1987:787). Thus, the Nile has not only been fundamental to Egypt's economy and well-being, it has also been a central part of the Egyptian identity.

Moreover, the fates of Egypt and Ethiopia have been closely linked. The Egyptian Abbas El-Tarabily wrote in 2002:

> I am just back from Ethiopia, the source of [84 per cent] of Nile water, which created Egypt. In fact, Egypt was born in Ethiopia and from the red mountains of Ethiopia came the water, which is the stuff of our life and the silt that created the fertility of Egyptian soil ... I was telling myself that it is from this place that the journey of the great river starts and carves the red rocks of Ethiopia leaving thousands of canyons and rifts that seemed to be the blood veins of the Egyptian body. (op. cit. Arsano 2007:73)

About 98 per cent of Egypt's fresh water comes from the Nile and there is practically no rainfall in Egypt. The Nile waters thus satisfy about 95 per cent of the country's various water requirements (Eleman 2010:219). Egypt argues that total rainfall in the Nile Basin is more than 1,600 bcm a year and it uses only 55.5 bcm of water from the Nile, and the country has no other options since it has hardly any rain. 'The Nile River is Egypt's principle artery of life. It is life itself for Egypt. This basic fact does not apply to the same extent to the other riparian states. Therefore, one of the major strategic threats to Egyptian national security is the threat to vital resources lying beyond Egyptian borders' (Hassan and Rasheedy 2011:131). Moreover, Egypt's water vulnerability is underscored by the fact that the country has the lowest rainfall of all the Nile Basin states (Hassan and Rasheedy 2011:135). As a country located in a desert and fundamentally dependent on the Nile, Egypt is extremely vulnerable to changes in water supply. Moreover, 'since population growth is the main reason that Egypt has reached its limits with respect to the availability of water from the Nile, further substantial growth in the population, in particular in rural areas, will be very difficult to cope with' (Elemam 2010:220). Increasing population growth has been a major concern in Egypt for a long time. Egypt established a family planning committee as early as 1966 with the aim of reducing fertility and thus population growth, and in 1995 a national population policy was implemented (Elemam 2010:220). According to the World Bank, the current population

(2012) in Egypt is 83.7 million and it is expected that by 2050 it will be between 130–140 million, which will put increased pressure on the resources of the Nile.

One fundamental challenge is that about 85 per cent of the water at Aswan comes from Ethiopia, which now has a population of more than 90 million. Ethiopia is called the 'Water Tower of Africa'. The annual rains provide Ethiopia with around 123 bcm of surface water annually, 1.5 times the annual water of the Nile. Nevertheless, Ethiopia has hardly used this water and most of the waters flow to the neighbouring countries – only 3 per cent of the water remains in the country (Arsano 2010:161). In Ethiopia, about 85 per cent of the population is agrarian and lives in rural areas. Ethiopia is among the poorest countries in the world, with only 5 per cent of the land suitable for irrigation developed. In 2010, Ethiopia was categorised by UNDP as a least developed country and ranked number 157 out of 169 countries. As much as 81 per cent of the population lives on less than US$ 2 a day (Oakland Institute 2011:4). Ethiopia has over recent decades experienced chronic food insecurity and in 2009 some 7.8 million (about 10 per cent of the population) were in the chronically hungry category. Ethiopia currently receives the most food aid in the world and when food prices spiked in 2008 an additional 6.4 million people became dependent on emergency food aid. In 2010, according to the Food Security Risk Index, Ethiopia was considered to be among the top 10 countries at extreme risk (Oakland Institute 2011:9–10). Thus, 'Ethiopia's consistent position has been that it must make use of its water resources in general and the Nile waters in particular to develop the impoverished country' (Arsano 2010:174).

In the 1950s, Haile Selassie stated:

> [I]t is of paramount importance to Ethiopia, a problem of the first order that the waters of the Nile be made to serve the life and the needs of our beloved people now living and those who will follow us in centuries to come. However, generally, Ethiopia may be prepared to share this tremendous God given wealth of hers with friendly nations neighbouring upon her, for the life and welfare of their people, it is Ethiopia's sacred duty to develop the great watershed which she possesses in the interests of her own rapidly expanding population and economy. To fulfil this task, we have arranged for the problem to be studied in all its aspects by experts in the field. Ethiopia has time and again set this forth as her position regarding the utilization of the Nile waters (op. cit. Arsano 2010:165–6).

Thus, the future prosperity of Ethiopia depends upon utilising more water resources, including the Blue Nile, Atbara and Sobat. Importantly, the increasing population is a major challenge for food security. The birth rate in Egypt (2009) was 2.8, whereas it was 4.4 in Ethiopia.[8] Egypt had a 1.7 per cent population growth in 2010, Ethiopia had 2.1 per cent.[9] Thus, future population growth in Egypt will seemingly flatten out after reaching some 130–140 million, whereas it will continue to increase in Ethiopia. Even so, with Egypt already experiencing acute water shortages with a population of some 80 million, an increase of 50–60 million people will drastically affect water availability and food security.

The need for more water is not restricted to Egypt and Ethiopia. In all Nile Basin countries there will be a dramatic population increase (see below). Consequently, there will be a greater need for water and food production. Sudan has not yet fully exploited the potential of the 1959 agreement for reasons of politics and civil war. Of its 18.5 bcm of water, only 12.5–14.5 bcm have been used and the rest has flowed into Egypt (Cascão 2009). However, this is about to change as Sudan plans new hydropower projects and irrigation schemes. The present government in Sudan developed a ten-year plan known as the Comprehensive National Strategy, 1992–2002, aimed at increased food security, sustained agricultural development, efficient resource utilisation and yield enhancement. The development of such new projects in Sudan has not only given rise to great concern in Egypt, which is accustomed to using Sudan's unutilised share under the 1959 agreement. The Sudanese government has estimated that the country will need 32 bcm of water by 2025 to meet food security and other needs (Taha 2010:207–9).

In other upstream countries and in the Lake Victoria region the situation differs and the needs and political priorities are both different and similar. However, since about 85 per cent of the water in the Nile at Aswan comes from Ethiopia, the main emphasis here is on Ethiopia, Sudan and Egypt. This is not intended to diminish the importance and role of water in the upstream countries, rather the contrary. The future development of all countries is dependent on using more water. However, given limitations of space and the complexity of each country's development and water uses, a superficial description would not be appropriate. Henceforth, I focus here on the common challenge all Nile Basin countries face with implications for water utilisation in the whole basin, namely population increase.

Population increase and poverty indexes

In the UN World Population Prospects for 2050 there are different figures depending upon whether low, medium or high scenarios are used. In this diagram

---

8. Source: World Bank. http://data.worldbank.org/indicator/SP.DYN.TFRT.IN (accessed 9 January 2012).
9. Source: World Bank. http://data.worldbank.org/indicator/SP.POP.GROW (accessed 9 January 2012).

medium scenarios are used, which predict the global population in 2050 to be 9.2 billion.

TABLE 2. POPULATION IN THE NILE BASIN COUNTRIES (UN PROJECTIONS)

Country	Population				
	1950	2009	2015	2025	2050
Burundi	2,456	8,303	9,413	11,161	14,846
DRC	12,184	66,020	77,419	98,123	147,512
Egypt	21,514	82,999	91,778	104,970	129,533
Eritrea	1,141	5,073	6,009	7,404	10,787
Ethiopia	18,434	82,825	96,237	119,822	173,811
Kenya	6,077	39,802	46,433	57,573	85,410
Rwanda	2,162	9,998	11,743	14,676	22,082
Sudan*	9,190	42,272	47,730	56,688	75,884
Tanzania	7,650	43,739	52,109	67,394	109,450
Uganda	5,158	32,710	39,710	53,406	91,271
Total	85,966	413,741	478,581	591,217	860,586

Source: UN 2009. World population prospects: The 2008 revision, pp. 6–10.
* South Sudan became independent in 2011. In the interests of compatibility and comparability, the data for total future population in both Sudan and South Sudan are combined.

The US census bureau has developed other statistics. In this case, expected population growth is slightly higher and the main difference is that the population of Ethiopia by 2050 is expected to be about 100 million more than in the UN projections.

TABLE 3. POPULATION IN THE NILE BASIN COUNTRIES (US PROJECTIONS)

Country	Population				
	1950	2009	2015	2025	2050
Burundi	2,363	9,511	11,574	15,465	27,149
DRC	13,569	68,016	79,375	99,162	144,805
Egypt	21,198	78,867	88,487	103,742	137,873
Eritrea	1,403	5,647	6,528	7,987	11,381
Ethiopia	20,175	85,237	103,134	140,140	278,283
Kenya	6,121	39,708	45,925	53,196	70,755
Rwanda	2,439	10,746	12,662	16,081	27,506
Sudan*	8,051	42,811	49,780	63,117	97,165
Tanzania	7,935	41,049	46,123	53,428	66,843
Uganda	5,522	32,370	39,941	56,745	128,008
Total	88,776	413,962	483,529	609,065	989,768

Source: US Census Bureau
http://www.census.gov/population/international/data/idb/country.php
* See Figure 2. In addition, future estimates for South Sudan are currently not available.

Although the predictions differ, the trend is similar and conclusive: there will be a dramatic population increase in the Nile Basin. Today there are more than 400 million people living in the Nile Basin countries. This will increase to about 600 million by 2025 and to 850 million or even as high as one billion by 2050. In a historic perspective, the population increase from 1950 to 2050 in all the Nile Basin countries will be tenfold. Exactly how many people will live in the catchment area is uncertain, but one may expect in the range of 400 to 600 million people. In practice, this means that the number of people dependent on the Nile and rainfall within the basin will double or triple from today. In short, this dramatic population growth will put immense pressure on water as a resource.

Moreover, this major population increase will take place in a region already haunted by poverty. According to the UN,

> Sub-Saharan Africa, in particular, remains mired in poverty. Its progress towards achieving the Millennium Development Goals lags behind that of other regions. The percentage of the population living in absolute poverty is essentially the same as it was 25 years ago. About 340 million Africans lack access to safe drinking water, and almost 500 million lack access to adequate sanitation. (UN Water 2009:xii)

Table 4 sets out the World Bank's statistics regarding rural population, poverty headcount ratio at national poverty line and GNI (Gross National Income) per capita in the Nile Basin countries.

TABLE 4. RURAL POPULATION, POVERTY HEADCOUNT RATIO AT NATIONAL POVERTY LINE AND GROSS NATIONAL INCOME PER CAPITA IN NILE BASIN COUNTRIES

	Rural population % in 2010 (1)	Poverty headcount ratio at national poverty line (% of population) (2)	GNI per capita, Atlas method (current US$) (3)
Burundi	89	66.9 (in 2006)	US$ 170
DRC	65	71.3 (in 2006)	US$ 180
Egypt	57	22.0 (in 2008)	US$ 2,420
Eritrea	78	69.0 (in 1993)	US$ 340
Ethiopia	82	38.9 (in 2005)	US$ 390
Kenya	78	45.9 (in 2005)	US$ 790
Rwanda	81	58.5 (in 2005)	US$ 520
Sudan	55	–	US$ 1270
Tanzania	74	33.4 (in 2007)	US$ 530
Uganda	87	24.5 (in 2009)	US$ 500

Source: (1) World Bank http://data.worldbank.org/indicator/SP.RUR.TOTL.ZS; (2) World Bank http://data.worldbank.org/country; (3) World Bank http://data.worldbank.org/country

According to the Human Development Report, only Egypt is classified as having medium human development while all the other Nile Basin states are classified as having low human development. Of all the countries in the world, Egypt is ranked as 113, Kenya 143, Tanzania 152, Uganda 161, Rwanda 166, Sudan 166, Ethiopia 174, Eritrea 177, Burundi 185 and at the very bottom of the list, DRC, at 187 (Human Development Report 2011:144–5). Thus, apart from Egypt, all Nile Basin countries are among the world's 45 poorest countries according to the multidimensional poverty index.

Before proceeding with the analysis, it is important to comment in general on these statistics. First, different countries have different poverty lines which makes direct comparison difficult. Second, in many cases coherent statistics are lacking, data are missing and several countries have no available statistics. Moreover, using GDP (Gross Domestic Product) and rates of GDP growth as measures of development is inadequate because this approach says nothing about the quality of the development (Lawrence, Meigh and Sullivan 2002:2).

As with the water stress indexes, there will always be uncertainties and divergent statistics. However, what is important is that many Nile Basin states are among the countries of the world with the highest poverty rates, most rapid population growth and increasing levels of water stress and/or scarcity. Water scarcity – low available water per capita – is forecast to worsen where population growth is still high (UN Water 2009:18), and between 2008 and 2100 more than 60 per cent of population growth will be in sub-Saharan Africa (32 per cent) and South Asia (30 per cent) (UN Water 2009:31). As emphasised in the Human Development Report (2006:163), the 'high level of pre-existing poverty and vulnerability' must be the starting point for all development discourse and for 'any evaluation of the threat posed by climate change in sub-Saharan Africa'. This cannot be limited to threats of climate change: 'Almost half of the region's population – some 300 million people – live on less than $1 a day. The majority live in rural areas, where income and employment depend almost entirely on rainfed agriculture. Sub-Saharan Africa already has a highly variable and unpredictable climate and is acutely vulnerable to floods and droughts'.

This ties in with the use of the Nile for irrigation projects aiming to enhance food production and thereby food security, which has been and still is a controversial issue.

CHAPTER 4 Agreements and disagreements

The colonial legacy

'The legacy of the colonial period is still relevant and still has an impact', Terje Tvedt says (Tvedt 2004:16). In order to understand the background to the 1929 and 1959 agreements, and consequently the disagreements about the Cooperative Framework Agreement, one has to turn to the colonial era because 'in the Nile basin the past is in the present and the present in the past, but nobody can escape the impact of the Nile's power and its history' (Tvedt 2004:326).

In his *The River Nile in the Age of the British. Political Ecology and the Quest for Economic Power* (2004), Tvedt analysed in detail how the British imperial policies regarding the Nile had the sole overall aim of securing British interests. Britain took direct control of Egypt in 1882. Small amounts of cotton produced in the delta were sold into a growing world market from the 1820s, but from the 1860s cotton exports made up about 80 per cent of Egypt's exports. British industry had huge economic interests in Egypt. The Lancashire textile industry aimed to reduce its dependence on American cotton and increase its supply of cheaper Egyptian cotton. To increase productivity and hence profits, more Nile water was needed at the right time – the 'timely season' or the summer season in Egypt. This is, however, before the annual Blue Nile floods and therefore cotton production was dependent on the waters of the White Nile. The overriding question was how to secure enough water for cotton production and at the same time control potentially devastating floods (Tvedt 2004:20–2). Thus, by the end of the 19th century, 'increased and improved water control was destined to top the agenda of any administration in Egypt' (Tvedt 2004:22).

The first Aswan Dam was completed in 1902. In 1894, British water engineers had published the *Report on Perennial Irrigation and Flood Protection in Egypt*, in which it was suggested that a reservoir be built at Aswan in Upper Egypt. The dam would be the biggest in the world. However, even at this early planning stage it was acknowledged that the dam would meet only half of Egypt's future needs and was only a temporary solution. Moreover, because of archaeological concerns that the dam would flood the pharaonic temples at Philae, the capacity of the dam was reduced by 50 per cent. Accordingly, in the mid-1890s it was believed the reservoir could not provide more than 25 per cent of Egypt's future water requirements. British water planners therefore looked further south beyond Egypt's borders to find a solution (Tvedt 2004:24–5).

Britain's colonial expansion in the Nile Basin was directly aimed at controlling the whole Nile and turning the Nile valley into a single planning unit. Since cotton production was dependent on the waters of the While Nile with peak demand in May, the marshes in southern Sudan were seen as a barrel filled with water of utmost importance to the British-controlled irrigation economy in Egypt. Only about half the water coming from Lake Victoria reached north of the swamp, and it was estimated that about 12 bcm of water was 'lost to evaporation'. William Garstin therefore proposed in 1899 and 1904 to build a 340 km long canal through the Sudd, which later was called the Jonglei Canal (Tvedt 2004:53, 67–8). From a British and downstream perspective, the White Nile was seen, as Garstin put it, as 'solely … the carrying channel which supplies Egypt with summer water', a perception of the Nile that has persisted until today (Tvedt 2004:79).

The British also saw the huge potential of developing irrigation schemes on the Gezira in Sudan. This is an enormous plain of about five million acres and would become the world's largest cotton farm, profiting Lancashire. However, if Sudan was going to develop, it needed more water, and quarrels over the Nile with Egypt were unavoidable. The Sennar Dam providing water to the Gezira Scheme was completed in 1925 (Tvedt 2004:105–6).

The use of Nile water was fundamental to Britain's colonial policy to control Egypt. On 22 November 1924, Lord Allenby announced his famous Nile ultimatum: 'The Sudan Government will increase the area to be irrigated in the Gezira from 300,000 feddans to an unlimited figure as need may require' (Tvedt 2004:110). This shocked and infuriated the Egyptian public, and in early 1925 Egyptian Prime Minister Ahmad Ziwar Pasha asked Allenby to revoke the ultimatum. After an exchange of notes, the British government committed itself to guaranteeing Egypt's future water supplies and compensating for the water taken at Sennar. This led to the Nile Waters Agreement of 1929, which stated that 'no irrigation or power works or measures are to be constructed or taken on the River Nile and its branches, or on the lakes from which it flows … in such a manner as to entail any prejudice to the interests of Egypt, either reduce the quantity of water arriving in Egypt, or modify the date of its arrival, or lower its level'. Contrary to what is often stated in the literature, the agreement did not specify the water rights in quantitative terms. It was, however, accompanied by the 1920 Nile Projects Commission report, where it was suggested that Egypt should be guaranteed water to irrigate up to 5 million feddans. On this basis, quantitative estimates were made giving Egypt rights to 48 bcm. Moreover, the entire flow of the Nile was reserved for Egypt in the dry season, whereas after 15 July Sudan was allowed to take water to the Gezira Scheme and fill up the Sennar Dam (Tvedt 2004:141–5). In practice, thus, this gave Egypt 48 bcm and Sudan 4 bcm, while 32 bcm flowed unutilised into the Mediterranean during the peak flow season.

Nile agreements

There were four agreements between the colonial powers: the Anglo-Italian protocol of 1891, the 1906 Tripartite Treaty between Britain, France and Italy, the 1906 agreement between the Belgian colonial authorities and Britain, and the 1925 Anglo-Italian agreement. Then there were agreements between colonial powers and basin states: the Anglo-Ethiopian Agreement of 1902, the 1929 Agreement and the Anglo-Egyptian Agreement of 1952. Finally, there were agreements between independent states in the Nile Basin: the 1959 Egyptian-Sudanese Agreement for the Full Utilisation of the Nile Waters, the 1993 Framework Agreement of the Nile Waters between Ethiopia and the Arab Republic of Egypt (Arsano 2007:95–104) and in 2010 the Cooperative Framework Agreement.

The 1929 agreement was made between Egypt and the British government, which signed on behalf of Sudan, Kenya, Tanganyika and Uganda. Before turning to the 1959 agreement, Ethiopia's position must be explored. Ethiopia was neither colonised nor part of the Nile Waters Agreement of 1929. Still, there is what is called a treaty of 15 May 1902. Britain had for decades tried to get permission to build a dam at Lake Tana as well as an agreement regarding the use of the Nile. The Ethiopian emperor signed a treaty with the British government, the English version of Article III of which reads (Tvedt 2004:114):

> His Majesty the Emperor Menelek II, King of Kings of Ethiopia, engages himself towards the Government of His Britannic Majesty not to construct or allow to be constructed, any work across the Blue Nile, Lake Tsana, or the Sobat which would arrest the flow of their waters into the Nile except in agreement with his Britannic Majesty's Government and the Government of the Soudan.

However, the 1902 agreement was never ratified by Ethiopia. Whereas in the English version Ethiopia was not supposed to 'arrest' the water, in the Amharic version a literal translation can be framed as follows: Ethiopia '… shall not block the waters from bank to bank' (Arsano 2007:97). The Amharic version thus had a different meaning and it was rejected by Menelik as an attempt to undermine Ethiopia's sovereignty (Kasimbazi 2010:721).

Sudan gained its independence on 1 January 1956. It subsequently declared a unilateral non-adherence policy towards the 1929 agreement, and was particularly concerned about the Aswan High Dam. Thus, with independence Sudan demanded more of the waters of the Nile, thereby jeopardising Egypt's plan to construct the Aswan High Dam. In response, Egypt mobilised troops at the Sudanese border (Arsano 2007:88). Tensions between Sudan and Egypt rose before the military takeover in Sudan in 1958, which enabled further negotiations over the utilisation of the Nile. On 8 November 1959, the agreement For the Full Utilisation of the Nile Waters was signed in Cairo between Egypt and Sudan, but not including the other riparian states (Waterbury 1979:70–2). Article 5 (2) states:

… as the riparian states, other than the two Republics, claim a share in the Nile waters, the two Republics have agreed that they shall jointly consider and reach one unified view regarding the said claims. And if the said consideration results in the acceptance of allotting an amount of the Nile water to one or the other of the said states, the accepted amount shall be deducted from the shares of the two Republics in equal parts, as calculated at Aswan.

As noted earlier, according to this agreement, of the annual average of 84 bcm of water as measured at Aswan, Egypt's share is 55.5 bcm and Sudan's 18.5 bcm, with the rest being lost to evaporation in Lake Nasser (Waterbury 1979:72–3).

Regarding the binding nature of the colonial Nile agreements, there are four main positions (Kasimbazi 2010:726–8). First, Egypt maintains that natural and historical rights are the basis for international law and that the other Nile riparian states are legally obliged to observe previous agreements. Moreover, adding to this position, in 1997 Egypt argued that colonial treaties and agreements are typically territorial treaties, and therefore states and their *successors* are bound and have to accept these legal obligations. Thus, 'territorial treaties' are not affected by the succession of states.

Second, when Sudan attained independence in January 1956, she refused to be automatically bound by former colonial treaties. Sudan argued that there had been a fundamental change of circumstances since the 1929 agreement and Egypt was eventually compelled to negotiate the 1959 Agreement with Sudan.

Third, Tanzania, Uganda and Kenya also rejected the former colonial treaties, but on different grounds. Tanzania's President Julius Nyerere formulated what has been known as 'the Nyerere Doctrine on state succession' in 1962. This doctrine considers colonial treaties as non-binding if they do not serve current state interests. With regard to Tanganyika, all former agreements with the UK ceased to exist and were terminated unless they were renegotiated within a two-year period. The doctrine explicitly rejected the 1929 agreement. Uganda also adopted this policy in 1962, as did Kenya following its independence in 1963.

Fourthly, there is Rwanda, Burundi and the Democratic Republic of Congo. When Rwanda became independent, it agreed to comply with international treaties and agreements made by Belgium, although the government was to decide which of these international agreements and treaties should apply to Rwanda. Burundi took more explicit steps regarding which agreements would prevail and on what conditions.

Finally, as regards Ethiopia, the 1902 agreement has never been ratified by Ethiopia and is not seen as binding on the country. Ethiopia was not part of the 1929 and 1959 agreements and as an independent country has never recognised them as being binding on Ethiopia's utilisation of the Nile.

Cooperative Framework Agreement

The Nile game has been dominated by three players – Egypt, Sudan and Ethiopia – with Sudan being the 'master of the middle'. However, being thus situated is not necessarily an advantage for Sudan. Egypt expects support from Sudan for its Nile policies and is interested in developing projects on the White Nile. On the other hand, 'the Sudan, with its tremendous potential for irrigated agriculture, is interested in exploiting this potential on a much greater scale; its priority is to pursue water-development projects on the Blue Nile, which would mean cooperating with Ethiopia', Fadwa Taha argues. She adds: 'If optimal water development were the overriding objective of Sudanese and Ethiopian policy-makers, they would have achieved close technical cooperation and joint projects decades ago' (Taha 2010:216).

Since the 1960s, several cooperative institutions like Hydromet (1967), Undugu (1983) and TeccoNile (1992) have been established. Their achievements have been limited because they did not include all riparian states and have focused on technical matters. In the 1990s, all Nile Basin states committed to developing a multilateral cooperative institution that would also address legal issues (Cascão 2009:246).

The Nile Basin Initiative was established in 1999. It had two main goals: to enhance socioeconomic development in riparian countries through sub-basin cooperation, and to strive towards a legal and institutional framework for regulating inter-state utilisation and management of the shared water resource (Arsano 2010:177). Specifically, it 'aimed to develop water resources of the Nile basin in a suitable and equitable way to ensure prosperity, security and peace for all its peoples; to ensure efficient water management and the optimal use of resources; to ensure cooperation and joint action between the riparian countries for their mutual benefit; and to eradicate poverty and promote economic integration' (Elemam 2010:229).

After a decade of negotiations, on 14 May 2010 Ethiopia, Tanzania, Uganda and Rwanda signed the new agreement, followed by Kenya on 19 May. The other countries were given a year to sign. Egypt and Sudan strongly opposed the agreement, but Burundi signed the agreement on 28 February 2011. Once Burundi signed, the necessary two-thirds of the Nile Basin states were onboard, making the agreement valid after ratification. The next step will be to establish a Nile River Basin Commission, which will oversee water development projects in the basin.

According to the new agreement, 'Nile Basin States shall in their respective territories utilize the water resources of the Nile River system and the Nile River Basin in an equitable and reasonable manner' and will abide by 'the principle of preventing the causing of significant harm to other States of the Nile River Basin'. The Cooperative Framework Agreement does not specify what such an equitable share of the Nile would involve and how much water can be used for different purposes by individual countries.

There are two controversies. One is Egypt's insistence that it has a historic right to the Nile that should be included in the new agreement. Sudan supported Egypt but the other upstream countries opposed Egypt's claim to historic rights. Teferra Beyene, head of transboundary river affairs for Ethiopia's ministry of water resources, said about the 1959 agreement with reference to the new agreement: 'We are not party to that agreement and we don't recognise it. We don't know of such a thing called historical rights. After all, this is going to be a new covenant, a new agreement among the riparian countries.'[10]

This sensitive issue of historic right centres on article 14b of the Cooperative Framework Agreement, which states that Nile Basin States agree not to 'significantly affect the water security of any other Nile Basin State'. Egypt and Sudan claim this compromises their share of the Nile and instead proposed the phrase 'not to adversely affect the water security and current uses and rights of any other Nile Basin State'. This would have acknowledged the 1959 agreement and given Egypt and Sudan historic rights.

The other controversy centres on how decisions are to be taken. Egypt and Sudan want decisions concerning the Nile Basin to be made by consensus and not majority vote, which in practice will give them, and in particular Egypt, veto power. Nevertheless, even without Egypt and Sudan, the Cooperative Framework Agreement has changed the geopolitical premises for the utilisation of the Nile by giving upstream countries a right to an equitable share and use of the water flowing through their respective territories.

New geopolitics – new challenges and premises

After Ethiopia, Tanzania, Uganda, Rwanda and Kenya signed the Cooperative Framework Agreement in May 2010, the Nile assumed even greater significance as a national security matter for Egypt. Within a week responsibility for further negotiations was transferred from the ministry of irrigation and water resources to the General Intelligence Services headed by its director, Omar Suleiman. Suleiman was later appointed vice-president of Egypt by Hosni Mubarak in the dramatic days before the Mubarak regime was overthrown on 11 February 2011.

It has often been claimed that the wars of the 21st century will be over water, not oil, and Egypt has previously threatened war if its Nile interests are jeopardised. These 'water war' scenarios will be discussed in more detail in Chapter 7.

Just before and after the Cooperative Framework Agreement was signed on 14 May 2010, the rhetoric adopted by Egyptian politicians was aggressive. Mo-

---

10. Egypt and Sudan continue to argue over the Nile, *Ethio Quest News,* 21 April 2010 http://www.ethioquestnews.com/The_Africans/Nile_Politics/Egypt_and_Sudan_continue_to_argue.html (accessed 23 May 2012).

hamed Nasreddin Allam, minister of irrigation and water resources, made a number of harsh statements in newspapers and to parliament in this period: 'The new treaty is not binding on us. It will only be an obligation for the countries that signed it. At the same time we will make sure that this treaty won't affect Egypt's share of the Nile's water.'[11] The vulnerability of Egypt was stressed: 'Ask the Egyptians to leave their culture and go and live in the desert because you need to take this water and to add it to other countries? No.'[12] He went on to stress Egypt's claim of historic rights to the Nile: 'Egypt's share of the Nile's water is a historic right that Egypt has defended throughout its history', and, 'We will not sign on to any agreement that does not clearly state and acknowledge our historical rights.'

Finally, he stressed the national security aspect of water for Egypt: 'Nile water is a matter of national security to Egypt. We won't under any circumstances allow our water rights to be jeopardized.'[13] He continued: 'Egypt reserves the right to take whatever course it sees suitable to safeguard its share.'[14] Similarly, prior to the signing of the agreement in May, Moufid Shehab, Egyptian minister of legal and parliamentary affairs, said that 'Egypt's historic rights to Nile waters are a matter of life and death. We will not compromise them.'[15] Former Defence Minister Field Marshal Mohammed Hussein Tantawi once remarked: 'Egypt's defence strategy was carved-out with a possible war over the Nile very much in our mind.'[16] In similar vein, one MP asserted in April 2010 that 'we welcome this war if it is imposed on us.'[17] In Sudan, Water Minister Kamal Ali Mohamed said in late June 2010: 'This agreement did not take into consideration all the views. Sudan and Egypt opposed the article regarding water security, which allows the rest of the countries that signed up to excessively use the Nile's waters.'[18]

---

11. *Al-Ahram Weekly*, 1–7 July 2010, Issue No. 1005, http://weekly.ahram.org.eg/2010/1005/eg4.htm (accessed 9 March 2012).

12. *Aljazeera*, 28 June 2010, http://www.aljazeera.com/news/middleeast/2010/06/201062871134786105.html (accessed 9 March 2012).

13. *Los Angeles Times World*, 20 April 2010, http://latimesblogs.latimes.com/babylonbeyond/2010/04/egypt-minister-rejects-nile-sharing-deal-as-experts-warn-of-water-famine.html (accessed 9 March 2012).

14. *Sudan Tribune*, 11 May 2010, http://www.sudantribune.com/Sudan-formally-rejects-the-Nile,35041 (accessed 9 March 2012).

15. Government of Southern Sudan Natural Resource Management Group, 29 April 2010, http://www.ssudan-nrmg.org/nrmg/index.php/nrnewssouthsudan/1-latest-news/216-wateranalysis-egypt-spat-fuels-water-tension-in-nile-basin (accessed 9 March 2012).

16. *Tigrai State,* 2 July 2010, http://tigraionline.blogspot.com/2010_07_01_archive.html (accessed 9 March 2012).

17. *Guardian*, 26 April 2010, http://www.guardian.co.uk/commentisfree/2010/apr/26/egypt-nile-water-negotiations (accessed 9 March 2012).

18. *Al-Ahram Weekly*, 1–7 July 2010, Issue No. 1005, http://weekly.ahram.org.eg/2010/1005/eg4.htm (accessed 9 March 2012).

The extent to which these pronouncements by Egyptian politicians were mainly rhetoric for domestic purposes or strategic negotiations or were real threats is difficult to judge.

In a notable twist of history, on 30 March 2011, just one and a half months after the fall of the Mubarak regime, Ethiopia announced its biggest ever project on the Blue Nile, the Grand Renaissance Dam at the border with Sudan. This 5,250 MW power plant will have a reservoir of more than 6 bcm. When it is completed in 2014, it will be Africa's largest and the world's tenth largest dam. The cost of the Renaissance Dam is Birr 80 billion or euro 3.3 billion (US$ 4.5 billion). Energy produced from the dam will be for domestic consumption as well as for export to Yemen, Djibouti, Kenya, Sudan and Egypt. Six other hydroelectric projects are also planned or under construction. According to the Ethiopian government, the projects developed over the next 10 years will produce 20,000 MW, and a total of US$ 12 billion will be invested over the next 25 years in the power infrastructure.

A mega-project of the scale of the Grand Renaissance Dam would normally have provoked strong reactions from Egypt, but the dam and the new regime in Egypt have changed the discourse on the Nile. It is uncertain what the current political situation in Egypt will imply for Egypt's future Nile negotiations, but the geopolitical premises have changed and aggressive rhetoric has given way to diplomatic dialogue and more conciliatory cooperation. This shift is captured in a statement by Hisham Kandil, Egyptian minister of irrigation and water resources, to a Nile Council of Ministers meeting in Nairobi in late July 2011 to the effect that Egyptians would 'look for ways and means to move forward because we have no other means but to cooperate and work together. We share the Nile, we share the water, we share the destiny and we know for sure that eventually we have to work together and let us not delay it. We have not delayed development and we very much support development.'[19]

The rhetoric surrounding the Cooperative Framework Agreement has also softened and the controversies over paragraph 14b have been downplayed. According to the Egyptian ambassador to Sweden, Osama Elmagdoub:

> We believe that we should find ways for upstream countries to benefit from the water and implement development projects without affecting the amount of water received by the other countries. Do we stick to 14b to the letter? I don't think it's necessary. We are not saying 'give us water and have scarcity'. That's not the approach. The approach is 'let's be fair'.

There are also similar approaches in Sudan. 'There is a point of difference on article 14b of the agreement', Kamal Ali Mohammed, Sudan's minister of irri-

---

19. Sudan Radio Service, 29 July 2011, http://www.sudanradio.org/egypt-open-cooperation-nile-basin-countries-nile-water-usage (accessed 9 March 2012).

Terje Oestigaard

gation and water resources said in August 2011. '[The upstream countries] took article 14b out of the legal framework and they are explicitly saying "we don't recognize your existing rights". We are trying to find a compromise on this.'[20]

'We all agree that the Nile is a bridge, it is not a barrier,' Ethiopian Prime Minister Meles Zenawi said in September 2011 at a press conference in Cairo. 'The future is a new relationship between Ethiopia and Egypt based on a win-win strategy. The past is a past based on a zero-sum game. That is gone. There is no going back.'[21]

Former Egyptian Prime Minister Essam Sharaf even went so far as to describe the planned Grand Renaissance Dam as a 'source of benefit'. 'We can make the issue of the Grand Renaissance Dam something useful', he said. 'This dam, in conjunction with the other dams, can be a path for development and construction between Ethiopia, Sudan and Egypt.'[22]

This change in tone is remarkable although one may wonder if it is part of a tactical diplomatic game. What is likely is that the uncertainty regarding the Nile issue will continue. Thus, the new geopolitical context together with predicted population growth and climate change that may make for a drier regime in the Nile Basin will ensure that in future the use of Nile waters will be more important for all countries. Moreover, with the independence of South Sudan in July 2011, there is also a new Nile Basin state with its own interests in Nile resources.

South Sudan

On 9 July 2011, South Sudan became an independent state. The area of the new state is about 640,000 square kilometres or approx. 26 per cent of the total area of former Sudan. According to the 2009 census, the population in South Sudan is approximately 8.2 million or 21 per cent of the total Sudan population of 39.1 million. Sudan has been devastated by civil war since independence in 1956 and the new state faces enormous challenges. Seventy five per cent of Sudan's documented oil reserves are now located in South Sudan, providing some 95 per cent of the South Sudan government's total income (Salman 2011:155–6).

The hydro-politics of South Sudan in years to come will be of utmost importance to the development of the country, but also to the Nile Basin region. About 90 per cent of South Sudan's territory is within the Nile Basin and about 20 per cent of the catchment area is within South Sudan. About 28 per cent of the Nile's waters or some 23 bcm as measured at Aswan flow through South Sudan. The White Nile coming from Lake Victoria contributes about 11.5 bcm

---

20. Châtel, F. and T. Oestigaard (2012), 'The Nile: Shifting Balance of Powers', Revolve: 32–9, p.35.
21. Ibid., p. 36.
22. Ibid.

or 14 per cent of the total Nile flow at Aswan, as does the Sobat River, which rises in Ethiopia before flowing to South Sudan, where it joins the White Nile (Salman 2011:157–8).

However, to date, although the government of South Sudan has jurisdiction over natural resources and forestry and local water-resource management, after independence jurisdiction over the Nile and transboundary waters is still in the hands of the government in Khartoum. It may seem counterintuitive that the Sudan People's Liberation Army/Movement did not push as hard for sovereignty over water resources and the Nile during the interim period from 2005 as it did for jurisdiction over oil and other natural resources. There may be two reasons for this. Firstly, the controversies over the Cooperative Framework Agreement: as we have seen, Egypt and Sudan strongly opposed this agreement, and the SPLM/A leaders may have feared that by becoming embroiled in the politics of the Nile involving several riparian states, they would jeopardise the prospects of sovereignty and independence for South Sudan or at least have complicated already complex and challenging negotiations. Second, in 2005 there were no functioning irrigation projects in South Sudan and for the time being the heavy rains have been sufficient for South Sudan's agricultural needs. Moreover, in the interim negotiations the Jonglei Canal Project was neither a priority nor an issue (Salman 2011:160–1).

Nevertheless, South Sudan is now demanding its share of water. Sudan has only been able to use about 14 bcm of the 18.5 bcm allocated to it in the 1959 agreement. Consequently, there should be water available for South Sudan. 5 July 2012 South Sudan was admitted as a full member to the Nile Basin Iniative.

On the other hand, with the loss of oil to South Sudan, Sudan now attaches more importance to agricultural development in its national economic strategy and will need more water (Salman 2011:162).

In Sudan, the Merowe Dam on the Nile, which opened in 2009, is currently the largest hydropower project in Africa (until the Grand Renaissance Dam is completed). Jebel Aulia Dam on the White Nile was completed in 1937. There are two dams on the Blue Nile: the Sennar, completed in 1925, and the Ro-seires, in 1966. In 2008, the Sudanese government signed a US$ 400 million contract with two Chinese firms to raise the Roseires Dam by 10 metres. The initial capacity of the dam was 3.4 bcm but silt accumulation has reduced this by 25 per cent. Heightening the dam will increase the reservoir capacity to 7.3 bcm, enabling more irrigation and hydropower.[23] As already noted, the total water needed by 2025 for Sudan's planned projects amounts to 32 bcm (Taha 2010:207).

---

23. *Sudan Tribune*, 28 April 2008.

The overall question thus remains – will there be enough water? There are two main considerations in this question: what hydrological impacts will climate change have on the Nile Basin and what agricultural developments will take place? It is to these issues we now turn.

Consequences of climate change

'Agriculture and rural development will bear the brunt of climate risk. This starting point matters because the rural sector accounts for about three-quarters of the people living on less than $1 a day ... Extreme poverty and malnutrition will increase as water insecurity increases' (Human Development Report 2006:159). Today, even without climate change, about 340 million Africans lack access to safe drinking water and almost 500 million lack access to adequate sanitation. It is estimated in the Intergovernmental Panel on Climate Change (IPCC) assessment report of 2001 that by 2020 between 75 and 250 million people in Africa will be exposed to increased water stress as a consequence of climate change, which will severely affect agricultural production (Holmberg 2008:7, 10). In particular, 'rainfed agricultural production, the source of livelihood for most of the world's poorest people, faces grave risks in many regions' (Human Development Report 2006:163).

A study conducted by the US Department of Agriculture estimated that 46 per cent of Africa's total land area is vulnerable to desertification or degradation, which is almost the total area of cultivable dryland. Degradation can be defined as 'loss of productivity' and starts with removal of vegetation (Holmberg 2008:23). Climate change is, therefore, expected to have severe effects on rainfed agriculture in sub-Saharan Africa: up to 12 per cent of cultivation potential may be lost by 2080, mostly in the Sudan-Sahelian zone (Rockström *et al.* 2007:328). By 2050, it is estimated that annual river run-off and water availability will be reduced by 10–30 per cent in dry regions and dry tropics and that rainfall in Africa will have declined by 5 per cent, as well as becoming more variable. As well, heavy precipitation is likely to increase, thereby increasing the risk of flood damage (Holmberg 2008:11). Higher temperatures will also accelerate evaporation from plants and soil. Some estimates suggest that the yields from rainfed agriculture in North Africa may be reduced by up to 50 per cent in the period 2000–2020 because of reduction in the growing season and increased heat stress (Toulmin 2010:57). This has a direct impact on economy and development. An Indian finance minister once said that his national budget was a 'gamble on the rains', highlighting the fact that 'variations in rainfall, or disruptions in water supply, can make the difference between adequate nutrition and hunger, health and sickness – and ultimately – life and death' (Human Development Report 2006:174). With greater fluctuations in rain patterns, this uncertainty and vulnerability will increase.

Agriculture and climate change are a two-edged sword – agriculture contributes significantly to carbon emissions. At a global scale, agriculture and land use contributes between 18 and 25 per cent to the world's carbon emissions, including tropical deforestation, which adds significant amounts of carbon (Toulmin 2010:68). In 2005, greenhouse gas emissions from agriculture accounted for 10–12 per cent the total emissions. Differing agricultural practices can reduce overall emissions and hence climate change, but it is unclear whether different or new agricultural practices can also meet projected food needs (Vermeulen *et al.* 2012:140). In some areas, climate change is expected to have a 'fertilising effect' due to global warming, resulting in increased yields. However, global warming is also expected to have the opposite effect in countries closer to the Equator, where increased temperatures will lead to decreased food crops and yields (Hanjra and Quereshi 2010:367) as a result of reduced soil fertility and increased attacks by pests, and also to decreased livestock productivity (Holmberg 2008:12). The consequences of extreme weather haunt poor countries and about three-quarters of natural disasters, such as drought or floods, are weather related. Moreover, 97 per cent of deaths resulting from natural disasters occur in poor countries (Holmberg 2008:15). Changes in night and day temperatures, precipitation rates, lengths and onset of growing seasons, and pest and disease build-up will affect agricultural productivity (Fresco 2009:379). In addition, 'climate-driven price fluctuations can lead to acute food insecurity for the relatively poor who spend most of their incomes on food' (Vermeulen *et al.* 2012:139). Climate change will have a severe impact on agriculture because first and foremost the changes will become manifest in water systems. Thus:

> Adaptation in the water sector is particularly critical. Having experienced one-third of all water-related disasters worldwide over the past ten years, Africa urgently needs a better management of water resources at all levels, including better management of major rivers, investment in irrigation and water-harvesting techniques, increased water storage at local level, and improved water access for domestic purposes. (Toulmin 2010:27)

Water systems

The IPCC defines climate change as 'a change in the state of the *climate* that can be identified (e.g., by using statistical tests) by changes in the mean and/or the variability of its properties, and that persists for an extended period, typically decades or longer'. It goes on to note that climate change may be due to natural internal processes or external factors, or to persistent anthropogenic changes in the composition of the atmosphere or in land use. The United Nations Framework Convention on Climate Change (UNFCCC), in Article 1, defines climate change as: 'a change of climate which is attributed directly or indirectly to human activity that alters the composition of the global atmosphere and which is in addition to natural climate variability observed over comparable time periods'. The UNFCCC thus distinguishes between climate change attributable to human activities and attributable to natural causes (IPPC 2007:78).

Nature, as perceived by humans, is to large extent different waterscapes. Different environments, whether they be deserts, savannas, tropical forests or arctic areas, are water-worlds or waterscapes, which change with the seasons and climatic variables. Following the hydrological cycle, precipitation is the climate element with the greatest socioeconomic importance. Societies and civilisations disappeared in the past partly because they were unable to adapt to new environmental circumstances and ecological variables. Changes in waterscapes have also given rise to new societal developments (Tvedt and Coopey 2010). These overall water-worlds constantly change in both the long and short term. Climate change is often perceived as long-term change (and often measured as changes over 30 years), but for humans these changes are also experienced as dramatic short-term events, such as prolonged droughts or sudden floods. Climate change and differences in water-worlds have crucial importance for the type of life-giving water in a given community. If water-worlds change, then the physical underpinnings of life change. Today, we live in an age when uncertainty about climate change has become an overriding issue. This uncertainty is primarily about the future of water. Are we living in a century that will see more floods, melting glaciers, heavier rainfall and increased sea-levels? Or will we see increased drought, less rainfall and shrinking rivers and lakes?[24]

Water is the basis of all agriculture. The absence or presence of different types of water sources, whether rain, river, lakes or a combination of water bodies, structures all societies. Too much water at the wrong time of year is as bad as too little water when it is really needed. This life-giving water is in a special category, because it is tied to the vital human need for a specific type of water at a particular time for agriculture and successful harvests. This is most often the annual flood or the rainy season (Oestigaard 2009).

Water systems in general can be understood to consist of three interconnected layers. The first layer addresses the physical form and behaviour of actual waterscapes. This can include precipitation, evaporation, how rivers run within the landscape and how much water they contain at a given time of the year; the relationship between rivers and the sea; and the development patterns to which these physical structures may give rise. Historically, variations in physical space have been of utmost importance to development. The second analytical layer addresses human modifications of and adaptations to actual water-worlds. The ways in which people in different societies have utilised water in the creation of social opportunity, and how modifications have reduced the physical constraints of water scarcity, have at all times structured societies and their future develop-

---

24. These issues were addressed at the conference 'The Age of Uncertainty: Climate change, water systems and social development', University of Bergen 16–18 February 2011, http://www.uib.no/geografi/en/konferanse/2010/11/the-age-of-uncertainty-climate-change-water-systems-and-social-development

ment. The third and final analytical layer addresses cultural concepts and ideas about water and water systems. Laws, management practices, control of water and ways in which humans engage with their water-worlds are intrinsic aspects of culture and cosmology. As a result, perceptions of water influence the technological use and development of water systems (Tvedt 2010a, 2010b).

Thus, there are three overall questions: First, will there be more or less water in the Nile owing to climate change? Second, how have different countries modified and adapted to the Nile River by changing the waterscape? Third, how do current and future management regimes impact the utilisation of the Nile's waters?

Level 1: The water in the Nile and the catchment area – today and in the future

How much water is there in the Nile River and will there be more or less rain in future and subsequently more or less water in the Nile?

In 2007, the total rainfall in the Nile Basin was estimated to be 1,745 bcm (and an annual water availability of 1,600 bcm is often mentioned). Of this total, an estimated 84 bcm makes up the average annual flow of the Nile at Aswan. This general figure is based on average measurements of the annual floods over a century. However, the annual amount of water varies significantly from year to year and the flood is dependent on the rains, particularly the wet season in the Ethiopian highlands. In 1878–79 (the 'water year' runs from flood to flood or from July to July), the total discharge was 150 bcm whereas in 1913–14 it was 42 bcm. In 1971–72 it was about 50 bcm but in 1975–76 it was twice that volume (Waterbury 1979:22). In 1984, the flow was estimated at 42 bcm (Molden, Awulachew and Conniff 2009:31).

At the Aswan High Dam, the Blue Nile contributes 57 per cent, the White Nile 29 per cent (of which 48 per cent comes from the Sobat in Ethiopia), and the Atbara River 14 per cent (Awulachew, Rebelo and Molden 2010:628). Taking a longer time span, from 1872–2002, the annual average flow of the Nile was estimated to be 88.2 bcm and the annual outflow from the Aswan High Dam from its completion to 2002 was 62.8 bcm (Awulachew, Rebelo and Molden 2010:629). As to the outflow into the Mediterranean, there are no certain estimates but they range from 9 to 30 bcm, and 9.8 bcm is estimated to be the minimum for securing aquatic ecosystems in the coastal region as well for leaching salt in the delta (Awulachew, Rebelo and Molden 2010:631). According to the World Bank, the amount flowing into the Mediterranean is about 12 bcm.[25] If this is correct, there are still some unutilised water resources. However, these numbers should be viewed with caution. As indicated previously, the 1959

---

25. http://www-wds.worldbank.org/external/default/WDSContentServer/WDSP/MNA/20
11/12/15/622B9D22AD5B2B7A85257967003D11D9/1_0/Rendered/PDF/P1180900PI-
D0Ap015201101323947221905.pdf (accessed 29 February 2012).

agreement allocated Egypt 55.5 bcm and Sudan 18.5 bcm, with about 10 bcm in estimated losses to evaporation, giving a total of 84 bcm. From this perspective, an outflow of 30 bcm seems much too high and it is also uncertain where the 10 bcm comes into the calculations.

The volume of water in the Nile depends on three factors: 1) annual precipitation, 2) run-off, and 3) evaporation, which is temperature sensitive.

Based on various measurements and analyses, since 1987–88 the Blue Nile flow has increased significantly while, by contrast, the flow of the White Nile has decreased since 1972–73. However, the overall water in the Nile has been fairly constant: '[T]his implies … that the decrease of the White Nile is counterbalanced by the increase of the Blue Nile and the Atbara flows' (Bushara and Abdelrahim 2010:19). The reduced contribution by the White Nile may result from climate change, since more water evaporates from the East African lakes and the Sudd. However, it seems that this evaporation falls as rain in the Blue Nile catchment area, thereby increasing the Blue Nile's flow (Bushara and Abdelrahim 2010:20).

Regarding the Blue Nile, Kim et al. (2008) have put forward one scenario suggesting that the climate in most of the upper Blue Nile River Basin will probably become wetter and warmer between 2040 and 2069. Based on six GCMs (Global Circulation Models) the mean annual precipitation will range from –11 per cent to +44 per cent (Kim et al. 2008:7). They concluded that 'the water resources of the Upper Nile River Basin may not be adversely affected by climate change unlike many other regions in the world and that increases in precipitation and associated water resources may help to meet future water needs in the region' (Kim et al. 2008:18). In another scenario, the expected change in annual precipitation in Ethiopia varied between –10 per cent and +25 per cent in 2050 (Elshamy et al. 2009:2). One simulation showed almost no changes between 2010 and 2099 whereas in another simulation, 'the annual flow at Dongola initially increases till around year 2040 then it is more or less stable until the middle of the 2060s. It starts a downward trend till the end of the century to reach only 61 per cent of the mean for the base period' (Elshamy et al. 2009:6).

Another interdisciplinary research group analysed the outputs of 17 GCMs for the Blue Nile for the period 2081–98.[26] The Upper Blue Nile basin covers an area of approx. 185,000 square kilometres. Mean average precipitation is generally between 1,200–1,300 mm, but the rain is highly seasonal and 70 per cent of rain falls from June to September. The study focused on the Upper Blue Nile at Diem, since about 60 per cent of the annual flow at Dongola originates there. Based on the GCMs, there was no consensus on future precipitation, which ranged from a 15 per cent decrease in rainfall to a 14 per cent increase.

26. The Nile Basin Research Programme's research group 'Climate in the Nile Basin Area', autumn 2007, at the University of Bergen.

Still, more models suggested a decrease than an increase in precipitation. Taken together, the models showed almost no change in rainfall patterns and only a slight reduction of 2.4 per cent in the wet season. However, with the predicted increase in temperature of between 2–5 degrees Celsius in the same period, there will be more evaporation and thus less run-off and consequently less water in the Nile (Elshamy *et al.* 2008). When all the models regarding run-off were taken together, they indicated that run-off would be reduced by about 3.5 per cent, which may result in about 15 per cent reduction of flow at Diem compared with today. However, the overall flow of water in the Nile is highly sensitive to rainfall patterns in different sub-basins, and some sub-basins may receive more rain than others.

Unfortunately, the models for predicting future precipitation are not precise enough at local and regional scales to provide secure analyses for the future, as these examples illustrate. Consequently, many uncertainties remain regarding climate change's effect on the water systems of the Nile Basin and the Nile's flow. Regarding the different scenarios, for each specific year in the future only one scenario can be the correct one. There might be more rainfall in some sub-basins and less in others, making future climate scenarios uncertain, especially as the same basins may in one period receive more rain and in a later period less. As a consequence, nobody knows if there will be more or less water in the Nile in the future.

Moreover, as has been pointed out, extended research on climate change does not necessarily lead to better knowledge, because more of the discourse takes place in political and cultural circles (Hulme 2009) that address themselves to how African countries adapt to climate change in general and develop their countries in particular. In the face of these uncertainties and different scenarios, policy planners ideally include two scenarios: there will be both more droughts *and* more floods and with greater frequency and intensity. When and where these will take place is uncertain. How is it possible to make policies which include both options? How is it possible to develop African countries in the face of climate change?[27]

The short answer, which is actual policy in many African countries, including those in the Nile Basin, is to build dams. Many African countries desperately need to improve their energy and food security. Dams provide both hydropower and store water for irrigation. Moreover, the reservoirs provide safety in years of low rainfall and drought and against devastating floods. Today, although building big dams is generally opposed by the West as unsustainable and undesirable, for many African countries this is one of the few feasible options, despite the high costs economically and otherwise (Oestigaard 2011a).

27. During the Stockholm World Water Week in 2011, there was a high-level ministerial panel of water ministers from Africa discussing this question.

Level 2: Modification and adaptation to changing waterscapes – human constructions and alterations of the hydrological world

Building dams for irrigation and hydropower has been the rule in the Nile Basin since the British colonial era and the construction of the first Aswan Dam in 1902, which was heightened in 1912 and 1933. Utilisation of the Nile was, as previously shown, intrinsically linked to cotton production, food production and national security concerns. In this section, three development projects that have shaped the Nile landscape in the past and will continue to do so will be briefly discussed. They are the Gezira Scheme, the Aswan High Dam and the Jonglei Canal, each illustrating three distinct ways of altering waterscapes: irrigation schemes for agriculture; dams and huge reservoirs; and directly changing the river's flow. All these human modifications are, of course, interrelated and tied to the overall question of how to secure as much water as possible for human utilisation.

Gezira Scheme

This scheme started in 1925 and it is still one of the largest irrigation systems in the world. It covers an area of 2.1 million feddan or about 880,000 hectares. However, it has also turned out to have general irrigation efficiency of less than 50 per cent, and accounts for about 35 per cent of Sudan's share of Nile waters under the 1959 agreement. There are approximately 120,000 farmers associated with the scheme, but they cannot earn a satisfactory income for their families from their crops (Government of Sudan and the World Bank 2000:1). Siltation of canals is a major problem. In many minor canals, siltation is so serious that little water reaches the tail end of the canals and consequently some areas are out of production. Moreover, there has been a general decline in silt removal from a peak 14.2 million cubic metres in 1995–96 to 6.9 million cubic metres in 1998–99. In the 1980s, when the canals were in a better condition and silt was regularly removed, between 5 and 7 million cubic metres was seen as satisfactory. In the 2000s, with canals in poorer condition, even the removal of 10–14 million cubic metres would not nearly suffice. Traditionally, weeds were removed manually, but health hazards such as bilharzia have led to the abandonment of this procedure. In 2000, only four of 20 excavators were operational and the operation and maintenance costs of removing silt and weeds were estimated to be approximately US$ 14.3/irrigable hectare (Government of Sudan and the World Bank 2000:10–11).

As the World Bank Report noted:

> The rules of the game when the Gezira Scheme was constructed by the British and subsequently under the management of Sudan's central government, were that the Scheme existed to produce cotton for export at the lowest possible cost.

This institution still exists. Quite often during the preparation of this report the suggestion that cotton should not be the core focus for the Scheme was rejected by the Gezira management. The rules of the game from the tenants' point of view were that if the Government wanted them to produce cotton the Government should provide all the support needed to do this at the lowest possible cost to the tenant. (Government of Sudan and the World Bank 2000:45)

Thus, once a major water system project has been developed, its impacts persist for decades and even centuries and have consequences for the future development of the Nile and its resources. In this regard it is also noteworthy that as part of the Gezira Scheme, dams were built on the Nile to supply the scheme with sufficient water at the right time.

Aswan High Dam

Dams have been seen as useful pyramids (Schnitter 1994), although control of the Nile was of utmost importance to the ancient Egyptian pharaohs, so that the building of the pyramids can also be seen in water perspective (Oestigaard 2011b). Dams are, however, massive human inventions. Indeed, the greatest human constructions in the world are in fact dams or other alterations to water systems.

When the Aswan High Dam in Egypt was inaugurated in 1971 it was one of the biggest dams in the world. The length at the crest of the Aswan High Dam is 3,600 metres and the height above bed level 111 metres. The total capacity of the reservoir is 162 bcm, and its length is 500 kilometres, with a surface area of around 5,000 square kilometres (Waterbury 1979:111).

Construction of the Aswan High Dam required 17 times more building mass than the Great Pyramid at Giza (Benedick 1979:123). The importance of the Aswan High Dam was described by Nasser in this way in 1958: 'For thousands of years the Great Pyramids of Egypt were foremost among the engineering marvels of the world. They ensured life after death to the Pharaohs. Tomorrow, the gigantic High Dam, more significant and seventeen times greater than the Pyramids, will provide a higher standard of living for all Egyptians' (Joesten 1960:59).

As Gamal Hamdan has remarked: 'The High Dam has simply eliminated the flood … It has converted the destructive river into a giant irrigation canal' (Waterbury 1979:87). The dam was constructed to store the equivalent two annual floods, so that if the floods in one year were disastrously low, Egypt would still have enough water until the next flood. The benefits of the Aswan high Dam were demonstrated in 1972 when the flood was one of the lowest in the century. Without the release of the waters behind the dam, over one-third of Egypt's harvest would have been lost (Benedick 1979:140).

Negatively, the construction of the dam has had a huge impact on the overall amount of water in the Nile reaching Egypt. The Lake Nasser reservoir is located in a desert at one of the warmest places on earth. Evaporation is estimated to be about 10 bcm or 12 per cent of the Nile's total annual volume, the equivalent of 2.7 metres depth of the reservoir each year. A projected temperature increase of between 3.2 to 3.6 degrees by 2080, together with other meteorological factors such as high wind speeds, will increase the rate of evaporation (Toulmin 2010:43).

This alteration of the Nile waterscape is, nevertheless, formidable. The old Aswan Dam could store about 6 per cent of average annual discharge (Waterbury 1979:88). The Sennar, Jebel Aulia, Khasshm El-Girba and Roseires dams have a total storage of 6.9 bcm (Cascão 2009:247). The other dams along the Nile could store less than 12 per cent, which meant that at least 80 per cent of each yearly flood (except for very low floods) had to be released downstream (Waterbury 1979:88–9). By comparison, the Lake Nasser reservoir can store two successive Nile floods. Still, even with such massive modification of the waterscape, there has not been enough water, and since the beginning of the 20th century there have been plans to divert the course of the Nile itself to gain more water.

Jonglei Canal and the Sudd

In South Sudan lie the massive swamps of the Sudd. The White Nile flows through the Sudd and it is estimated that the outflow of water (on average, 14 bcm annually) from the Sudd is only about half the inflow at Mongalla (27 bcm), the rest being lost to evaporation (Jonglei Investigation Team 1953:35).

From a downstream perspective, the enormous loss of water in the Sudd has been a concern since colonial times. One of the Nile Equatorial Project's primary objects was 'to hold back the flood until it is required for irrigation purposes farther north. This is what is called "annual storage", in other words control of the river to suit irrigation requirements at any given time in any one year. A further and even more important objective is to control the water so as to ensure that these requirements are met not only in any year, but also every year' (Jonglei Investigation Team 1953:35–7). The plan had long been to dig a canal to bypass the Sudd area, which became known as the Jonglei Diversion Canal. The first plan for constructing such a canal was proposed by William Garstin in 1899 and 1904 (Tvedt 2004:68). Based on measurements in the first half of the 20th century, such a canal would increase the water supply below the swamps from the present average 14.2 bcm to 22 bcm, a gain of 7.8 bcm, of which 6.9 bcm would be available for the timely season (Jonglei Investigation Team 1953:38–9).

Actual construction of the Jonglei Canal first started in 1978 and the design was substantially based on Garstin's original proposal. There would be 360 kilometres of canal from Bahr el Jebel at Jonglei village to the confluence of the White Nile and the Sobat River. The costs were estimated at US$ 260 million and the costs and benefits were to be divided between Egypt and Sudan. When completed, the canal would provide an additional 5 bcm of water to the White Nile. Another planned canal was to drain a large part of the remaining swamps in the area of Bahr el Jebel and Bahr el Zeraf. Other studies indicated that from Bahr el Ghazal and the Machar/Sobat swamps a similar amount of water could be drained. Altogether, these four projects could almost double the White Nile's flow (Salman 2011:163).

However, the Jonglei Canal Project faced huge resistance in southern Sudan because it served only the interests of Sudan and Egypt. By November 1983, 260 kilometres of the Jonglei Canal had been completed, but in February 1984 the SPLM/A attacked the canal site and since then the canal has turned into a large ditch (Salman 2011:163).

Level 3: Laws, management practices and cultural control of water

These interventions in the Nile waterscape testify to the stakes involved in the negotiation of the Cooperative Framework Agreement. The use and utilisation of the Nile was regulated and controlled by Egypt and Sudan in the 1929 and 1959 agreements. In the past, there has been great concern about controlling and enhancing the water in the Nile for irrigation and hydropower. Today, these concerns are shared by all Nile Basin states and with the Cooperative Framework Agreement Sudan and Egypt are no longer the only players in the management of the Nile. Given anticipated climate changes and their impact on hydrological systems in the Nile Basin, although nobody knows for sure what these will be, there is an ever greater need for all Nile Basin states to secure their water resources. In practice, as the politics unfold, this amounts to building more dams and developing irrigation schemes.

Irrigation potential and plans

Not only is food production the largest consumer of water, it is also the biggest unknown regarding future global water demand. First, it is difficult to predict how changing diets in countries and regions will affect water demand. Second, the production of biofuels, with its competing demands for water and land, is also uncertain. Third, improved water technology may enhance productivity (more crop per drop), but at what pace and where is uncertain. And finally, the impact of climate change on how much water will be available where and when is uncertain (UN Water 2012:25).

With increased populations, how is it possible to share the Nile equitably? The question regarding the use of water for hydropower is easier to answer than that regarding water for irrigation. With hydropower, the water will be sent downstream, but with a delay. Irrigation, on the other hand, uses the water and there will be less water left in the tributaries and eventually in the Nile.

In sub-Saharan Africa, 95 per cent of agriculture is rainfed. This represents a huge uncertainty, since plenty or famine is dependent on the arrival of seasonal rains at the right time and in the right amount. Moreover, if climate change results in less rain, rainfed agriculture will be exposed to greater vulnerability and risk. One way to reduce this vulnerability is by developing irrigation schemes, which make agriculture more productive and predictable.

The importance of this is underscored by poverty mapping, which shows the highest poverty within the basin to be 'where people are highly dependent upon rainfed agriculture and have limited access to managed water. Irrigated crop-livestock systems show low vulnerability while pastoral, agropastoral and mixed rainfed production systems exhibit high vulnerability to water related hazards' (Awulachew, Rebelo and Molden 2010:648). Thus, although irrigation has often been associated with environmental degradation and sometimes adverse social impacts, it is still one of the most crucial agricultural inputs contributing to poverty reduction, stable and affordable food prices and improvements in livelihood practices. The main reason for this is that average irrigated yields are 60 per cent higher than yields from rainfed agriculture (Rosegrant *et al.* 2009:206).

From 1985 onwards, there was a sharp decline in lending by the World Bank to irrigation and drainage projects, mainly for four reasons. First, at that time there was a sharp decline in cereal prices. Second, it was recognised that many irrigation schemes had performed poorly. Third, the costs of irrigation construction were increasing (although they are now declining) and fourth, there was increased opposition to large dam projects because of the associated environmental degradation and social displacement (Molden *et al.* 2007:74). However, irrigation will continue to have a crucial role in the world's agricultural production.

It is anticipated that the area under irrigation in sub-Saharan Africa will double by 2050, but will still only account for some 2 per cent of global irrigated area (Rosegrant *et al.* 2009:207). In the Nile countries, on average only 2.8 per cent of arable land is irrigated (with the exception of Egypt, which has 100 per cent irrigated cropland, and to a lesser degree Sudan), while only 3.8 per cent of arable land in the other sub-Saharan countries is irrigated. This is considerably lower than in, for instance, South Asia, where 30–40 per cent is irrigated (Molden, Awulachew and Conniff 2009:68). Regarding land use in the Nile Basin, food produced by rainfed crops covers four times as much land as food produced from irrigated crops – 23 and 5 million hectares respectively (Molden, Awulachew and Conniff 2009:37).

Importantly, the total irrigation potential of the Nile Basin is 8 million hectares (FAO 2005:26), of which some 5.5 million are currently irrigated. In practice, this means that there are limited land and water resources for future irrigation schemes in the Nile Basin. Still, 'most governments prefer irrigation as a water intervention because of its capacity to raise productivity and reduce vulnerability' (Awulachew, Rebelo and Molden 2010:648). Thus, where and when will the irrigation schemes be developed?

In Egypt in 2002, 3,422,178 hectares were under irrigation and the total irrigation potential is estimated to be 4.42 million hectares. If Egypt proceeds with all its planned projects on the Upper Nile, it will require 9 bcm more water (FAO 2005:200–3). In Sudan before South Sudan became independent, total arable land was estimated at about 105 million hectares and in 2002 16.65 million hectares or 16 per cent of arable land was used for agriculture. The total area equipped for irrigation was 1.863 million hectares in 2000 (FAO 2005:527). Apart from Egypt and Sudan, Ethiopia is the only other Nile Basin country with irrigated agriculture, but it is insignificant compared to the other two countries. 'However, the potential to develop irrigated agriculture in Ethiopia is significant' (Molden, Awulachew and Conniff 2009:15).

There are several different scenarios regarding Ethiopia's irrigation potential and actual development plans. It is the official policy of the Ethiopian government to develop agriculture to eliminate the country's dependence on food aid. Ethiopia has the potential for more than 2.5 million hectares of irrigated agriculture and has huge plans to develop both small-and large scale agriculture of this sort. The potential for irrigation in the three Nile headwater basins of Ethiopia is 1,496,00 hectares, which is about 58 per cent of the country's total potential. Some surveys and reports put Ethiopia's maximum irrigation potential at about 5.7 million hectares (Awulachew and Ayana 2011), although the more common estimate is about 3.6 million. At present, given land and water availability, technology and finance, the irrigation potential is estimated to be about 2.7 million hectares. In 2001, the area under actual irrigation was said to be about 290,000 hectares or approximately 11 per cent of the potential. Traditional irrigation schemes were estimated to account for about 138,000 hectares, modern small-scale irrigation schemes about 483,00 hectares, modern private irrigation about 5,500 hectares and public irrigation schemes about 97,700 hectares (FAO 2005:224–6).

Published information on water use in Ethiopia is not available, but agriculture is estimated to account for fully 94 per cent of such use. Annual water use in agriculture is thought to be about 5.2 bcm based on total irrigation area and cropping patterns (FAO 2005:223). Ethiopia plans to develop about 275,000 hectares of irrigation schemes by 2016. With these developments, the annual agricultural water use is expected to increase from 5.2 bcm to 9 bcm (FAO 2005:232).

Although there are uncertainties about the statistics and the feasibility of the planned irrigation projects, the conclusion with regard to water use is clear: 'Not all the ambitious plans to expand irrigation in the long-term development scenario are possible with the available water resources, infrastructure and current water management' (Awulachew, Rebelo and Molden 2010:648). Taking the different national plans for irrigation development (including small-scale irrigation) in the Nile Basin as a whole, the area under irrigation will increase from today's total 5.5 million hectares to 7.9 million hectares in the medium term and 10.6 million hectares in the long term, almost double today's irrigated area. However, these figures are uncertain in that they depend on the adoption of advanced technologies and changes from conventional irrigation. Moreover, most of these plans are based on surface water and do not take into consideration renewable ground water or rainwater management. Thus, Awulachew, Rebelo and Molden (2010: 645–6) found that more large-scale irrigation is possible, but not at the levels planned. 'At the current level of water application and irrigation efficiency, and in the absence of reservoir management, the total water requirement for the long term scenario ... would be 127 km^3. For the medium-term scenario, ... 94,5 km^3, still higher than the 84,1 km^3 (1900–50 average) and the 88,2 km^3 (long term average) available.'

Thus, the future plans for total irrigation development in the basin exceed the actual volume of water in the Nile for use in irrigation, particularly as 'water availability in the Nile river system was found to decrease for the medium-term and long-term scenarios as compared to the current scenario' (Molden, Awulachew and Conniff 2009:80). Although the Cooperative Framework Agreement proposes that Nile Basin states will use water resources in an equitable and reasonable manner 'following the principle of preventing the causing of significant harm to other States of the Nile River Basin', there is always a risk that 'all national development plans made by one government concerning the use of the Nile will be perceived by another as a threat to its national interests and thus a source of international conflict' (Hultin 1995:38). Can all parties be winners in this competition for the Nile? Even if Egypt and Sudan develop new irrigation schemes before Ethiopia, what will happen if Ethiopia develops its full irrigation potential and hence reduces overall water flow to Sudan and Egypt?

The general solution can be summarised thus:

> While there is scope for some irrigation expansion, in order to come close to future plans, mitigation measures are required that include improvements in water productivity, increase the storage capacity upstream to reduce evaporation in downstream storage, enhanced carry over storage, and implement demand management and water saving practices. (Molden, Awulachew and Conniff 2009:83)

The majority of the people and farmers in the Nile Basin will still rely on rainfed agriculture in future. However, as is often pointed out, 'water for agriculture is not well exploited in the rainfed systems' (Awulachew, Rebelo and Molden 2010:648). Even so, rainfed agriculture will be more important than irrigation because improvements in rainfed agriculture have been largely neglected and the potential for new irrigation is limited (CGAAER 2012:12). The proposed solution is increased water productivity and upgrading rainfed areas, which includes expanding rainfed croplands. This also necessitates new and improved surface water storage facilities (Fraiture and Wichelns 2009:101). Improved rainwater harvesting techniques will undoubtedly be of utmost importance, in particular for subsistence farmers living on the bare minimum. However, improved water harvesting techniques will of necessity reduce the amount of water in the Nile, because run-off will be less.

Another proposed solution is ethical: changing consumers' habits by eating more grain and less meat, and ideally, going vegetarian, 'and [by] reducing energy intensive lifestyles, [which] offers the best hope to tackle climate change and food security issues' (Hanjra and Quereshi 2010:372). From a global or Western perspective, this may sound like a solution, but it is hardly a real option for African farmers. On one hand, the majority is already living in absolute poverty and, on the other, increased living standards, if they eventuate, will result in changing and more water-intensive diets. Therefore, if successful farmers are able to escape the poverty trap and afford a more varied, nutritious and healthy diet, returning to their previous life is not development. Consequently, the most important way to mitigate climate change and assure food production in agriculture is by producing more crops from less land (and water) (Vermeulen *et al.* 2012:140). One way to achieve this is by making irrigation systems more efficient.

Irrigation efficiency in Egypt

In 2002, the total irrigation area in Egypt was 3,422,178 hectares. Of this, 3,028,853 and 171,910 hectares were respectively under surface and sprinkler irrigation in the year 2000. Surface irrigation is banned by law in newly reclaimed areas and sprinkler and drip irrigation, if efficiently used, need less water than surface irrigation (FAO 2005:203). In Egypt, irrigated agriculture contributes about 17 per cent to the country's GDP and employs about 31 per cent of the labour force (Gohar and Ward 2011:737). Of the 55.5 billion cubic metres of Nile water that is allocated to Egypt every year, about 85 per cent is used for agriculture.

Egypt's irrigation is generally seen as notoriously inefficient. Agriculture in Egypt could increase in efficiency and its contribution to national income through the better allocation of water among crops, seasons and locations (Gohar and Ward 2011:755).

How efficient are irrigation systems? This is a controversial issue with significant political implications. Traditionally, efficiency is measured as the irrigation water consumed by the crops divided by the losses (apart from the leaching required to control salinity). For instance, based on the classic irrigation efficiency measurement, if efficiency is 50 per cent, the implication is that 50 per cent is lost. Keller and Keller, for instance, argue that if 50 per cent of water delivered is lost to crop evapotranspiration, the remaining 50 per cent is not lost but most of it flows to surface and subsurface areas. This return flow is most often captured by downstream users (see the criticism of this approach below). Thus, 'one user's inefficiency can be the next users' supply of water. When the water is reused, the overall basin-wide efficiency increases. Thus, the irrigation system as a whole can be much more efficient than any of its parts' (Keller and Keller 1995:7). To address this methodological problem and evaluate the efficiency of an irrigation system as a whole, they proposed the concept of 'effective irrigation efficiency'.

They use Egypt's Nile Valley irrigation system to illustrate the difference between understanding irrigation efficiency through 'classic efficiency' models and 'effective efficiency' models. In the lower valley, the salinity is about 365 ppm. Consequently, sustainable irrigation requires outflow leaching of 8.2 per cent and effective outflow of the actual outflow is 91.8 per cent. Classic irrigation efficiency measures, when used in the Grand Valley, yield an efficiency estimate of only 41.2 per cent, suggesting that there are significant opportunities to reduce what appears to be a loss of water (Keller and Keller 1995:17). Other estimates vary between 35 and 45 per cent (Keller, Keller and Davids 1998:153). However, the remaining water is reused, and the effective irrigation efficiency is actually 91.3 per cent, which is high. Thus, in the valley there are small opportunities to save water when the system is seen as a whole (Keller and Keller 1995:17). About one-third of irrigated agriculture is in the valley and the remaining two-thirds in the Delta and the 'lost' water in the valley is reused in the Delta. Based on the above estimates, effective efficiency in the Delta will probably be in the range of 60 to 65 per cent. Similarly, most of the return flow in the Upper Delta is reused in the Lower Delta and consequently the greatest potential for water savings in

Egypt will be in the Lower Delta reaches, before the water flows to the Mediterranean (Keller, Keller and Davids 1998:153).

> In closing river systems, it is important to be able to identify and quantify real water savings that can be used to transfer water to other areas, or to increase productivity of the existing area. The concept of effective efficiency, which accounts for the quantity and quality of both the supply water and the return water from each irrigation use cycle, provides a basis for quantifying real water savings: real water saving will result wherever the effective efficiency of irrigation is increased. (Keller, Keller and Davids 1998:161)

Thus, from a catchment area perspective and using this approach, in Egypt as a whole there are small possibilities to save water in irrigation at an overall level. However, this explanatory model also has political implications (or can be used politically in one way or other). One may easily get the impression that due to run-off, Egypt has sufficient water for irrigation and that only small improvements are possible or needed because the water is reused downstream. This is not necessarily so. Egypt is located in a desert with extreme temperatures and evaporation is high. Thus, one may question how much water actually flows downstream and is reused. This also relates to the length of time the water is exposed to heat and evaporation in irrigation channels and the rate of the flow. Moreover, pollution is a severe problem, making much of the water unfit for cultivation further downstream.

Egypt is a highly water-stressed country today, and the use of water for agriculture also draws attention to the types of crops being cultivated. Cotton is the most important natural fibre in textile industries worldwide, accounting for about 40 per cent of textile production, whereas synthetic fibres account for about 55 per cent. Between 1997 and 2001, trade in cotton products amounted to 2 per cent of the value of global merchandise trade. Of the earth's arable land, 2.4 per cent is used for cotton production and the global water footprint of growing and processing cotton is 2.6 per cent. Average virtual water use of seed cotton is 3,644 cubic metres/ton and global water use for cotton crops averages 198 Gm^3 (Chapagain et al. 2005:15).

In the period 1997–2001, Egypt produced an average 710,259 tons of seed cotton using an estimated 4,231 cubic metres/ton of water (Chapagain et al. 2005:15). This means that total Egyptian cotton cultivation requires about 30 bcm of water each year. Cotton production is thus highly water-consumptive, which also impacts the environment, quite apart from pollution. As a comparative example, between 1960 and 2000 the Aral Sea lost approximately 60 per cent of its area and 80 per cent of its water volume thanks to irrigation schemes producing cotton (Chapagain et al. 2005:10). Moreover, Egypt is the second largest producer of sugar in Africa, with an estimated production of 1.8 million tons in 2008–09 (Food Outlook 2010:35). Egypt also produced 21 million tons of cereals in 2010, and imported 14 about million tons (Food Outlook 2010:62).

Thus, there is a huge imbalance between producing water-thirsty export crops and cultivating low water-intensive food crops. This is, however, also a question of how individual farmers and states fit into the global market. As indicated earlier, there may be good reason for farmers not to grow food in the short run even if they risk starvation. This situation relates to the possible profits obtainable from irrigated agriculture on the world market, irrespective of the water use or water footprint on a national or global scale. Cotton is not the only water-intensive crop that generates a much needed income for a large number of people: sugar, rice and vegetables are also important agricultural products. With an increasing poverty rate, the net difference between growing cash crops and subsistence crops is vital to individual farmers and households (see discussion below), although it may not be sustainable in the long (or short) run in terms of water use or national food security. This in turn draws our attention to the types of crops that should be grown on irrigation schemes: high value cash crops or food crops requiring little water?

Irrigation costs and benefits

Development of irrigation schemes requires huge investments, but such schemes are still the preferred development path for many Nile Basin countries. Thus, it is necessary to examine the costs and benefits of irrigation. Inocencio *et al.* (2007) analysed 314 irrigation projects implemented between 1967 and 2003 in 50 countries in Africa, Asia and Latin America in order to address the general assumption that irrigation projects in sub-Saharan Africa are more expensive than elsewhere. The World Bank has estimated that the average cost of irrigation projects in Africa as a whole is US$ 13,000 per hectare, whereas in sub-Saharan Africa the figure is US$ 18,000 per hectare. This is in stark contrast to South Asia and East Asia, where the averages are US$1,400 per hectare or US$ 4,000 per hectare respectively (Inocencio *et al.* 2007:1). Based on their investigations, they came up with, however, other and lower total unit costs 'defined as the total irrigation-related project costs divided by the project size' (Inocencio *et al.* 2007:17). The total unit costs in sub-Saharan Africa for new construction projects and rehabilitation projects were US$ 14,500 and US$ 8,200 respectively (Inocencio *et al.* 2007:18). However, these high figures must be qualified.

Irrigation projects in sub-Saharan Africa are not inherently more expensive than in other regions and there are two main reasons for these high figures. First, in sub-Saharan countries many of the irrigation projects are new constructions and therefore cost more than rehabilitation of older structures (Inocencio *et al.* 2007:18). Second, the costs include both successful and 'failed' projects. Sub-Saharan Africa has a high rate of 'failed' projects, with costs of US$ 23,200 per hectare. The successful projects, however, have a cost of only US$ 6,000 per hectare (Inocencio *et al.* 2007:20–1). Thus, although irrigation projects are more expensive in sub-Saharan Africa, the costs of successful projects are not that much higher than in other regions.

Moreover, many of the most costly failed irrigation projects were built in the 1970s and 1980s. In the 1970s, almost 60 per cent of the irrigation projects failed whereas in the 1990s the success rate increased to almost 90 per cent. Importantly, developing irrigation in the later stages is less expensive than it was earlier because of advances in technology (Inocencio *et al.* 2007:26–7). Based on the success of projects in recent years, Inocencio *et al* came up with two other important insights, which at first glance may seem contradictory. On the one hand, project size matters: the larger the project, the lower the unit cost. Hence, for irrigation projects 'big is beautiful' (Inocencio *et al.* 2007:33). On the other hand, smaller irrigation systems have a higher performance, particularly where farmers actively participate in the process and have a sense of partnership and ownership (Inocencio *et al.* 2007:37). Finally, the team also demonstrated that the probability of successful irrigation projects is higher if they are combined with power projects (Inocencio *et al.* 2007:29). Thus, they conclude that 'big projects are better, but big projects supporting small-scale irrigation systems may be the best' (Inocencio *et al.* 2007:42).

In order to create economic growth and reduce poverty, and hence make progress in achieving the MDGs, the Ethiopian government has identified the Lake Tana catchment area as key for the development of hydropower structures and irrigation schemes. The mean depth of Lake Tana is nine metres, with a maximum of depth 14 metres. At the outlet of the lake, the catchment area is 15,321 square kilometres. The total estimated cultivable land is 517,500 hectares, but there is less than 500 hectares under small-scale irrigation and no large-scale irrigation at all. Apart from hydropower projects, irrigation schemes for up to 60,000 hectares are planned along the main rivers flowing into the lake, of which the Ribb is the largest. If all the plans come to fruition, they will divert about 3.6 bcm from the lake. As a consequence the mean annual level will decrease by 0.44 metres and the surface area decline by 30 square kilometres and up to 81 square kilometres during dry seasons. They will also lead to severe environmental degradation (Alemayehu, McCartney and Kebede 2010, see also McCartney *et al.* 2010).

The cost of developing irrigation in Ethiopia is considerably higher than in, for instance, Egypt, where mobile sprinkler irrigation and stationary sprinkler irrigation cost about US$ 800/hectare and US$ 1,800/hectare respectively (FAO 2005:205). In Ethiopia, small-scale irrigation schemes cost US$ 1,760–2,940 per hectare for direct diversion from rivers and US$ 4,700–7,100 per hectare if micro-dams are required. In 1998, large and medium public surface irrigation schemes were estimated to cost in the range of US$ 3,300–12,800/hectare, with an average of US$ 8,100/ha. The main reason for the high costs of developing irrigation in Ethiopia is that the construction of expensive headworks is included (FAO 2005:228).

Despite the high investment costs, there are sound economic reasons for such irrigation schemes, in addition to the greater food security compared to rainfed agriculture. In 2005–06, irrigation generated an average income of US$ 323/hectare, while the gross margin for rainfed agriculture was US$ 147/hectare. In other words, the gross margin for irrigation is more than double that for rainfed agriculture (Hagos *et al.* 2009:12). The average income from modern medium-scale irrigation was US$ 400/hectare, whereas the average income from large-scale irrigation schemes was US$ 1,456/hectare. Moreover, sugarcane schemes had a generally higher annual income than schemes involving other crops, including outputs per unit of land and water use as compared with fruits, vegetables and cotton (Hagos *et al.* 2009:13). Compared to the annual average of US$ 147 from rainfed agriculture, the net difference per hectare compared to large-scale irrigation schemes is US$ 1,308 in favour of the latter. Where the per hectare returns for large-scale irrigation differentiate between sugar plantations and other crops, the average net income is US$ 1782.5 and US$ 998.9 respectively (Hagos *et al.* 2009:14). One driver behind this agro-development is thus sugar prices, which have tripled over the past five years.

Thus, on one hand developing irrigation schemes is highly expensive, and, on the other, large-scale irrigation, particularly for sugar cultivation, produces substantial income. On the global market the costs and the benefits meet, and Ethiopia may serve as an example. How can poor countries develop their agricultural sector quickly?

In the last few years, there has been a large increase in demand for land for agro-industrial production. Ethiopia is one of the few key recipients in Africa of foreign direct investments in land. In 2010, the total land assigned for biofuel production was 1.5 to 2 million hectares (including land that was cultivated, assigned or under negotiation). The ministry of agriculture has recently indicated that Ethiopia will in addition lease out about 3 million hectares of farmland over the next five years for purposes that will include biofuel production (Beyene 2011:93).

According to the Oakland Institute, about 3.6 million hectares have been granted to investors, and different reports estimate that between 3.6 and 4.5 million hectares have been made available for commercial land investment (Oakland Institute 2011:18, 21).

This area of land is larger than or equal to the area of irrigable land in Ethiopia. In Sudan and South Sudan 4,9 million hectares have been leased out to foreign investors since 2006. Although it is uncertain how much land will be put under production in practice, these areas need water for irrigation (Grain 2012).

Recently, it has become a stronger awareness that land grabbing to a large extent may be motivated by the desire to capture water resources, and hence named 'water-grabbing' (see Mehta *et al.* 2012).

In a Nile Basin perspective, how much of the land to be leased out will be part of irrigation schemes is uncertain, but foreign investors investing in biofuels are unlikely to invest in low producing areas dependent on unpredictable rainfall. Thus, will Nile waters be used to produce food so as to enhance food security in the Nile Basin, or to produce biofuel and energy for the global market?

Agricultural land and biofuel

Under the influence of the World Bank, small household farming has in many places been replaced by large-scale agriculture, which is believed to be more competitive (Havnevik *et al.* 2007). The role of the World Bank and the IMF in the globalisation process in Africa has been to promote a 'move away from insufficient production structures and to concentrate resources in the branches that have a comparative advantage, and hence increase the growth rate of the economy' (Lundahl 2004:14), although many of these projects have largely failed. African agriculture has thus developed along two main trajectories. On one hand, there is smallholder farming often dependent on rainfed agriculture where the emphasis is on diversity and, on the other, large-scale monoculture farming dependent on the market, which also favours biofuel production (Matondi, Havnevik and Beyene 2011:15).

Global plans to partly replace fossil fuel with biofuel (biodiesel and bio-ethanol) are massive. India plans to replace 20 per cent of petrodiesel with biodiesel, while China sought to have 15 per cent of transportation using biofuel by 2010. The US plans to produce 36 billion gallons of biofuel from corn and cellulose crops in 2022 and the EU aims to replace 10 per cent of existing transport fuels with biofuel by 2020 (Gerbens-Leenes and Hoekstra 2011:2658). By 2020, it is estimated that around 400 million tons of grains will be burned as biofuel, which equals the total world rice harvest. This will put increased pressure on global food prices (Hanjra and Quereshi 2010:372).

In 2010, the World Bank conservatively estimated that each year until 2030 about 6 million hectares of additional land will be brought into biofuel production, of which some 4 million hectares will be in sub-Saharan Africa and Latin America (Matondi, Havnevik and Beyene 2011:3). It has been estimated that over the past decade about 230 million hectares of land have been the subject of international deals in developing countries. Africa is the prime target for such deals and in this period an area twice the size of France was sold or leased.[28]

---

28. Interview with Kjell Havnevik by Lina Lorentz, p. 28 in L. Lorentz (2012), 'Global rush for land puts smallholders at risk', *NAI Annual Report* 2011: 28–29, Nordic Africa Institute, Uppsala.

Land acquisition or land grabbing in Africa is often based on the mistaken assumption that there is abundant underutilised land (and water resources) available. This is a grave misconception because even though there are marginal agricultural areas, no external, private or Western profit-driven investors will target marginal or degraded land. There are higher profits in fertile areas with sufficient water resources that are close to the markets (Matondi, Havnevik and Beyene 2011:7–8).

This has direct implications for food production and water use, because Africa 'badly needs to raise food production, create employment and reduce consumer prices (while low in absolute terms, food prices are often high relative to income). This requires continued investments in, and support for, agriculture' (Matondi, Havnevik and Beyene 2011:15). In the words of the *World Development Report 2008*:

> Although large-scale agriculture has a place in some land-abundant areas of Africa – if it is driven by markets rather than subsidies and if the rights of the current land users are adequately protected – it would be a grave mistake to forsake the proven power of smallholders to jump-start growth, reduce poverty, and solve the hunger crisis in Africa and beyond. Promoting smallholder farming is not 'romantic populism' but sound economic policy. (op. cit. Havnevik 2011:41)

This is, however, in stark contrast with what seems to be happening in Africa. According to Palmer (2010:5):

> Mozambique's Minister of Energy, Salvador Namburete, for example, stated that '36 million hectares of arable land could be used for biofuels without threatening food production, while another 41 million hectares of marginal land would be suitable for raising jatropha'; Zambia's Minister of Agriculture, Brian Chituwo, boasted 'we have well over 30 million hectares of land that is [begging] to be utilised'; while his counterpart in Ethiopia, Abeda Deressa, suggested that pastoralists displaced by land grabbing 'can just go somewhere else'.

Much can be said about this, but as the Oakland Institute has pointed out with regard to land-grabbing for biofuel production in Ethiopia , 'villagization and displacement of people, the loss of farmland, the degradation and destruction of natural resources, and the reduction of water supplies are expected to result in the loss of livelihoods of affected communities'. The consequences will include 'change in diet, loss of traditional lands, increased reliance on wage employment and aid, and weakened community bonds' (Oakland Institute 2011:38).

Thus, 'the expansion of cash-crop monocultures has a severe impact on local availability of food, as it diverts food-producing resources and labour to cash-crop production. As a result, communities are forced to depend on the market, putting them at the mercy of volatile food prices' (Matondi, Havnevik and Beyene 2011b:185). Apart from the social and economic consequences, a central issue is how land acquisition, and in particular land-grabbing for biofuel production, will affect transboundary water management and domestic water supply (Jägerskog, Cascao, Hårsmar and Kim 2012).

From a water perspective, the energy derived from biofuel has a water footprint 40–70 times greater than that for fossil fuels. In producing one litre of biofuel, evaporation ranging between 2,500–3,500 litres occurs, about the same amount of evapotranspiration required to produce the daily food for one person (approx. 3,000 litres) (Fraiture and Wichelns 2010:504). In short, one litre of biofuel uses the same amount of water as food for a person for a day. How much water future biofuel production will require is uncertain, but estimates range from 1,000 km^3 to 11,700 km^3 (Fraiture and Wichelns 2010:504).

The higher estimates of water consumption in biofuel production are alarming from a global food security perspective. As already indicated, the amount of crop water consumption is expected to increase by 70–90 per cent by 2050 to between 12,050 to 13,500 km^3, compared with today's 7,130 km^3 (Fraiture and Wichelens 2007:99). In other words, in the worst-case scenario the amount of water needed to produce enough food for the world's population equals the amount of water needed for future biofuel production. Since water is a finite resource, there will most likely be increased competition in future over water for food or fuel. In addition, increasing urbanisation will also lead to higher competition for water and it is expected that withdrawals for non-agricultural sectors will have more than doubled by 2050 (Fraiture and Wichelens 2007:103). Moreover, 'African governments have consistently failed to invest in agriculture, despite an earlier commitment to allocate at least 10 per cent of national budgets to this sector' (Toulmin 2010:64–5). Thus, one may ask whether biofuel production is the right agricultural investment, given that food security will be of greater concern in the future.

From a Nile Basin perspective, such concerns add another global dimension. The tensions between Egypt and Ethiopia over utilisation of the Nile waters have, as previously shown, led to threats of war. Today's surge and pressure on Ethiopian land for biofuel production comes mainly from Indian companies (Oakland Institute 2011:22). Thus, potential conflicts between Egypt and Ethiopia over the Nile may be driven or intensified by other global actors, in this case the energy market. From an African perspective, this could be a repeat of the exploitation of resources and warfare associated with the colonial 'Scramble for Africa'.

On the other hand, is this development in agriculture where fertile land is used to grow cash-generating products for the world market benefiting both individual farmers and nation states? Given the logic of capitalism, with increased income farmers in areas with little water and growing stress on water resources may buy food and their daily necessities on the global market. This is also the consequence of the logic of trading food in terms of 'virtual water', which has been presented as a solution to many of the problems discussed above.

CHAPTER 7 Virtual water, water wars and water riots

Virtual water – a solution or part of the problem?

The concept of 'virtual water' has been developed by Tony Allan in a number of works (Allen 1996, 1998, 2002, 2003, 2011) and subsequently by others. The idea is simple and has gained significant political influence. Water is used in all food production. Virtual water is the water needed for agricultural production. It takes about 1,000 cubic metres to produce one ton of grain. Grains require little water compared to other agricultural products. Beef production, for instance, in which cattle often are fed grains, is water intensive: it is estimated that 1 kilogram of beef requires 15,000 litres of water to produce. Thus, beef has a water footprint 15 times greater than grains (or grass): in other words, the amount of water needed to produce 1 kilogram of beef could produce 15 kilograms of grain. Consequently, by producing low water-intensive crops such as grain, it is possible to feed more mouths than by producing high water-intensive products such as beef. Moreover, the idea is that water-poor countries should (or could) import food and commodities from areas with abundant water resources, so that nations 'save' their own water. From this perspective, water is an international currency.

In global water discourse, this has two political consequences. On the one hand, to produce enough food for the growing population on earth it is necessary through better water management to use less water in agricultural production. Importantly, and this is where the concept of virtual water has gained greatest momentum and has the greatest political implications, where does the agricultural production take place? To save water locally, nationally and globally, the idea is that it is beneficial to produce food in water-rich areas and then export food to water-poor or scarce areas, thereby 'saving' water. The Middle East and North Africa (MENA) region is water scarce, and by the turn of the millennium this region imported at least 50 million tons of grain annually. Given that about 1,000 litres of water is needed to produce one ton of grain, from a 'virtual water' perspective the region by this means saves 50 bcm of water, more or less equal to Egypt's share of Nile water as defined in the 1959 agreement (Allan 2003:5). Still, it is food that is traded, not water, but by importing a ton of wheat a community is released 'from having to harness 1,000 tons of its own water', and this 'imported' water can thus be called 'virtual water' (Allen 2002:256).

So far so good, and it looks good on paper. But, as critics have asked, does such a concept work in practice and have relevance for political processes and decisions? And does it contribute to water saving on local, national and global levels? Allan uses the concept 'virtual water' in relation to agricultural production only, but as he argues, it is possible to extend it to other activities and water uses as well (Allan 2002:5). However, since about 70 per cent of the earth's fresh water is used in agriculture, this sector has the greatest potential impacts.

Does 'virtual water' as a concept work? As long as there is trade in food, the short answer is yes. However, Fraiture *et al.* (2004) have analysed the impact of virtual water trade on global water use, and their conclusion is that one should be cautious about emphasising the importance of trade to global food security and water-use mitigation (Fraiture *et al.* 2004). There are several reasons for this.

First, if virtual water trade is truly efficient, there has to be a net difference in water use between importer and exporter. Water savings occur if countries with favourable rain-fed conditions export food to water-scarce countries mainly by using irrigation or if they have more efficient water production systems. In 1995, total cereal production in the world was about 1,724 million tons, of which 13 per cent or about 215 million tons were traded. The imported 215 million tons would have depleted 433 bcm of crop water and 178 bcm of irrigated water if grown in other places. Because of production differences between importers and exporters, globally water use was reduced by 164 bcm of crop water and 112 bcm of irrigation water, which means that, without trade, the global crop water use in cereal production would have been 6 per cent higher and irrigation depletion 11 per cent higher respectively. Together, without trade, global crop water use would have been 9 per cent higher in 1995. In 2025, without trade the water depleted in irrigation is estimated to be 19 per cent higher (Fraiture *et al.* 2004:24). Thus, the importance of virtual water will be rather modest in the future.

Second, the US is the largest cereals exporter, accounting for about half of all cereal exports. In the world, there are five main regions where cereals are grown under favourable rain-fed conditions: US, Canada, Argentina, Australia and EU. These regions account for about 80 per cent of food exports worldwide. There are about 25 main importers in Asia, the Middle East and Africa, among them Egypt (Fraiture *et al.* 2004:8–9). However, most food trade is unrelated to global water scarcity and takes place for reasons unrelated to water: the bulk of the trade takes place between rich countries and countries that are water abundant (Fraiture *et al.* 2004:v, 25).

Third, there is a difference between water 'saved' at a national level and water 'saved' globally. There are cases where the importer is more water sufficient than the exporter, so that there is an increase in water use. Indonesia imported 2.3 million tons of grain from India in 1995. If Indonesia had produced these grains itself, 16.7 bcm of water would have been used. India, however, used 17.4 bcm, so that this trade increased global water use by 0.7 bcm (Fraiture *et al.* 2004:12).

Fourth, Egypt is a main importer of grain. In 1995, Egypt imported 7.9 million tons, mainly from the US and EU, which would have required some 9.9 bcm of irrigated water (Fraiture *et al.* 2004:11). The real question is whether Egypt 'saved' 10 bcm? In 2000, Egypt's total water withdrawal was estimated at 68.3 bcm: 61.27 bcm from the Nile Basin, 7.043 bcm through groundwater extraction and 0.825 bcm from the eastern and western deserts, mainly the Nubian sandstone aquifer (FAO 2005:2002). In 2007, the World Bank calculated in the MENA Development Report (2007:166) that Egypt has 16.0353 bcm virtual water imports in crops and 2.897 bcm in livelistock. Egypt thus imported food products that would have required an additional 19 bcm of water. In sum, Egypt's actual water use (about 68 bcm) plus imported agricultural products represent water use amounting to 87 bcm, which is more than the annual flow of the Nile. In regions with scarce water resources, international trade in food is often presented as a way for a nation to 'save' water. However, to call this 19 bcm 'water saving' may be misleading, because Egypt does not have these water resources in the first place and lower imports would in practice mean starvation or fewer Egyptians (Fraiture *et al.* 2004:25).

Fifth, trade and virtual water is hardly an option for Sub-Saharan countries as a major development path because of the very premise upon which it rests: trade and fluctuating prices on the global marked. Thus, one of the main problems with 'virtual water' and imports of agricultural products as a means to 'save' a country's water is that many poor countries, in particular in sub-Saharan Africa, do not have sufficient exports to finance such imports (Fraiture and Wichelns 2010:508). If they do not have other high-value resources, they are totally dependent on agriculture. Also, food security will then depend on the international market where food imports have to be paid for in foreign currency and which may be subject to increasing prices and varying availability.

Sixth, virtual water analyses have generally omitted the substantial costs of shipping large volumes of food between countries and continents. With increasing energy prices, the costs per unit of processing, storing and transporting food will increase (Fraiture and Wichelens 2007:123). In addition, numerous sub-Saharan Africa countries, including Nile Basin countries, are landlocked. Being landlocked implies severe constraints on market access and transport costs are generally very high since most people cannot use rivers as waterways (Bigsten and Durevall 2008:34–5). The net result will be a further increase in the food prices for countries that are already among the poorest in the world.

In an article entitled 'Virtual water and water footprints offer limited insight regarding important policy questions' (2010), Wichelns extends the criticism mainly by highlighting that most virtual water approaches do not consider opportunity costs. Why should an individual and poor farmer care about global 'water footprints'? An important aspect is that farm-level decisions regarding water use are not necessarily optimal from a society's perspective, let alone a global perspective. It is at first glance a paradox that many water-scarce countries produce water-intensive products like fruit, vegetables and cotton, which are exported, and then import cereals requiring smaller amounts of water. The arid Andalusia region of Spain is one such region, as is Egypt, which produces world-class cotton for export. If one were to follow the rationale behind virtual water, it would be much better for these regions, Egypt included, to produce cereals and import fruits, vegetables and cotton. The obvious reason for this anomaly is that the prices for fruits, vegetables and cotton are higher than for grains (Wichelns 2010:643–4).

Based on ongoing research in Tanzania (Oestigaard in prep.), for individual farmers, whether rich or poor, it makes sense to generate as much income as possible by cultivating crops that can be sold on domestic or international markets and then to buy cereals at the same markets. From a poor farmer's perspective, however, there are no cheap cereals. In today's world, everyone needs money and volatile and increasing food prices make the need to generate more income ever more urgent. When the poor are barely able to make ends meet – and in most cases they can't – there is only a marginal net difference between selling cash crops and buying life's necessities. This net difference is, however small, vital particularly to farmers in sub-Saharan Africa living on an absolute subsistence minimum. Thus, even in arid regions farmers depending on fluctuating rainfall patterns may choose to grow water-intensive crops well aware of the fact that if the rains fail, they are left with nothing. If they had chosen crops requiring less water, they could have some harvest even in years of bad rain and consequently some food. Subsistence farming means living on the absolute minimum – in other words, in extreme poverty and often starving. The possible net difference if rains and harvests are successful is a calculated reward and risk that comes at a high price. However, very few farmers take the risk of planting only cash crops (Oestigaard 2012).

In rural areas in Uganda, Tanzania and Kenya, as elsewhere, farmers and households try to diversify their livelihood systems in the best way they can to minimise risk from what they perceive as increasing weather variability (Vermeulen et al. 2012:140).

> Pasture-fed and free roaming livestock do not use additional blue water, and in many places animals graze where no other form of agriculture can take place. Moreover, for many malnourished people livestock products are important for a balanced diet, while livestock rearing and fisheries are extremely important livelihood activities for many poor people. (Molden et al. 2007:80)

In particular, in rainfed agriculture diversifying risks is the best guarantee for survival as well as generating a minimum income.

Importantly, farmers depending on rainfed agriculture have limited choices and opportunities. Cultivating some cash crops is one way of trying to make ends meet. There is nevertheless the matter of scale in any discussion of food trade and 'virtual water'. Although sugar, jatropha, cotton and to some extent rice are sold and part of the global market, the food bought for subsistence is mainly locally produced. Thus, the global trade in water and food is not applicable to the majority of farmers in sub-Saharan Africa because the money they can earn from cash crops is so minimal that it provides only temporary relief: there is virtually no way they could base the whole of their subsistence and existence on imported food. If they could escape poverty by buying food produced for and bought on the world market, they would have done so long ago. Nobody wants to live in poverty (Oestigaard in prep).

This is perhaps the most important shortcoming of water footprint and virtual water perspectives: the almost total neglect of agriculture as a livelihood for people (Wichelns 2010:647). Even with increased urbanisation, in sub-Saharan Africa agriculture and rural life will remain the main source of livelihood for about 70 per cent of the population.

Producing food and food security is therefore and will continue to be an overall aim for farmers in sub-Saharan Africa. Moreover, development in agriculture has the greatest potential for poverty alleviation. In poor countries, growth in agriculture is more than five times as effective in reducing poverty among the poorest than development in other sectors. Indeed, in sub-Saharan Africa it may even be more than ten times more efficient among the poorest (Hårsmar 2010).

'It is not sufficient to know the water footprint of coffee, tea or pizza without also knowing the opportunity cost and livelihood implications of water allocation and use in production regions,' wrote Wichelns (2010:649). In other words, these general theories may look good on paper and on a global scale, but have little relevance for sub-Saharan farmers depending on rainfed agriculture, who have few alternatives other than trying to survive on their own harvests. 'In sum, virtual water and water footprint calculations are essentially silent on the most important aspects of water allocation and use' (Wichelns 2010:649). Thus, 'virtual water' and food trade do not represent a solution to the water and food scarcity the Nile Basin region faces today, which in all likelihood will increase in the future.

In defence of Allan's concept of 'virtual water', however, one may add that it was mainly developed as an analytical tool for understanding why there have not been any 'water wars' in the Middle East (2003). The underlying premise is that acute water and food scarcity may lead a nation to war over water, the basic necessity for all life and the well-being of any state and its inhabitants. This has not happened and the notion that water scarcity will lead to water wars is too simplistic because it only focuses on the supply side and not on social and political issues related to water (Ravnborg 2004:5). Allan's argument has been that it is because states have been able to handle water shortages by importing food from elsewhere that they have been able avoid escalating conflicts over water, which could lead to wars. Still, 'water wars' are frequently debated.

Egypt and water wars

The Middle East, in particular the Nile, has been identified as a hot-spot where war over water is likely to be fought in the 21st century. Boutros Boutros-Ghali, Egypt's foreign minister in the 1980s, predicted in 1988 that the next war in the Middle East would be fought over 'the waters of the Nile, not politics' (Bosire 2011:194). Ismail Serageldin, the vice-president of the World Bank, said in 1995 that 'many of the wars of this century were about oil, but wars of the next century will be about water'.[29] And in March 2001, UN Secretary General Kofi Annan reiterated these sentiments, but in February 2002 he also stressed that 'the water problems of our world need not be only a cause of tension; they can also be a catalyst for cooperation ... If we work together, a secure and sustainable water future can be ours' (Carius, Dabelko and Wolf 2004:60). The change in dialogue related to the Cooperative Framework Agreement may be an example of water as a source of both conflict and cooperation. Even so, what will happen in the Nile Basin region is uncertain and conflicts may erupt.

There is good reason that water war scenarios have been proposed in the Middle East and over the Nile's waters. All of Egypt is dependent on the Nile.

> The Nile River will always be the defining influence of Egyptian foreign policy towards the states in the basin region. The issue of the Nile River water and its significance for the survival of the people in Egypt has been clear in the minds of all political leaders in Cairo to the extent that there has been no significant difference among the successive administrations over the decades. (Hassan and Rasheedy 2011:149)

In May 1978, Egyptian President Sadat warned: 'We depend upon the Nile 100 percent in our life, so if anyone, at any moment thinks to deprive us of our life we shall never hesitate [to go to war] because it is a matter of life or death' (Waterbury 1979:78). In 1979 Sadat reiterated that 'the only matter that could take Egypt to war again is water', and Egypt has threatened Ethiopia with war on numerous occasions. In 1977, for instance, when Ethiopia planned to divert water from the Blue Nile for irrigation schemes in response to frequent droughts and famines, Sadat declared that if Ethiopia proceeded, 'there is no alternative to use our force. We will retaliate when something happens but we have to be ready with plans and alternatives to firmly stop any action' (Adar 2011:182–3). Moreover, although relations between Egypt and Sudan regarding the utilisation of the Nile have generally been cooperative, Egypt has nevertheless on several occasions threatened military force against Sudan to protect Egypt's interests in the Nile's waters (Deng 2011:39). President Mubarak, for instance, once said: 'those who play with fire in Khartoum ... will push us to confrontation and

---

29. *New York Times*, 10 August 1995.

to defend our rights and our lives' (Deng 2011:51). In fact, Deng argues, 'Egypt has issued ... more threats against Sudan than against any other country of the Nile Basin. Hence, the duality is more ... an Egyptian imposition that the Sudanese regimes bitterly swallow, lest they become easy prey to Egyptian political manipulations and plots' (Deng 2011:52–3).

The security of the Nile has been central in Egyptian military planning. Other riparian users of the Nile have been seen as a national security threat to Egypt.

> As deterrence, the Egyptian High Command has established contingency plans for armed intervention, in each country in the Nile Basin, in case of a direct threat to the flow of the Nile. Egyptian military plans, known as *Waraa-el-hidoud*, were traditionally associated with Nile water. Some of the plans date back to the early nineteenth century, to the days when Mohammed Ali was rebuilding the Egyptian army. All have been updated several times since then, several by the British around the turn of the century. Today, a full-time staff at Nasser Military Academy in East Cairo reviews and adapts the plans to changing circumstances. (Yacob 2004:2)

There can be no doubt Egypt has the military muscle to go to war against other Nile Basin states. As an example, Egypt's military expenditure in 2005 was more than twice the equivalent expenditure of all the nine other riparian states together (Adar 2011:183).

A possible but likely scenario?

Across the world, there are 263 international rivers. Based on a comprehensive survey, Wolf *et al.* have analysed 1,831 episodes of conflict or cooperation in relation to these waters: 507 were found to be associated with conflict, 1,228 were cooperative and 96 were neutral or insignificant (Wolf *et al.* 2003:33). In modern times, there has been no war over water resources, and one has to go back 4,500 years to find a true 'water war'. This took place between the city states of Lagash and Umma on the Tigris-Euphrates. Most interactions are cooperative and when there are conflicts, the level of conflict is mild (Wolf *et al.* 2003:38–9).

However, there is a war that has been called a 'water war'. In 1894, Britain took control of the Great Lakes in Africa and the headwaters of the White Nile, a fate that Sudan also shared. In 1896, Kitchener with an army of 20,000 soldiers and a flotilla of gunboats crushed the Mahdist regime in Sudan. The then war correspondent Winston Churchill dubbed this the 'River War' (Churchill 1933). By controlling Sudan and the lake region, Britain controlled the Nile from its headwaters to Suez (Tvedt 2010c).

As Tvedt argues, however, with regard to the question of whether water scarcity will lead to interstate conflict or cooperation, 'the relationship between water and international politics is so complex that abstract models or general either/or questions are not very useful.' He continues: 'A definite physical position in a river basin, be it as an upstream or a downstream power, will definitively tend to make some patterns of actions more likely ... but the actors will at the same time (but not always) have a wide range of possibilities, between outright competition and full cooperation' (Tvedt 2010c:78). Moreover, cooperation and conflict may occur simultaneously in a basin (Jägerskog and Zeiton 2009).

The 'water war' scenario has nevertheless gained great popular coverage in the media, but is it likely? Wolf argues that there are at least four reasons why water wars might be unlikely: 1) an historic argument, 2) a strategic interest argument, 3) a shared interest argument and 4) an institutional resiliency argument. He further asks what would be the goal of launching a war over water? In other words, how is it possible to win a water war? If the object is to destroy a dam, the destruction would result in a wall of water rushing downstream, creating havoc and deluge. If the project is quality-related, either industrial or waste treatment, destroying such structures will probably worsen water quality downstream. If the issue is water depletion through irrigation, the occupying force would have to not only conquer the area but depopulate the entire catchment. And for what purpose, Wolf asks? A water war will be extremely costly and involve extremely difficult operations over access to and control of a resource that could be achieved more easily and cheaply by desalinating sea water at about US$ 1 per cubic metre (Wolf 1998). Today, indeed, this price has dropped to US$ 0.5–0.8 (Shippers 2012:82).

Importantly, however, as Wolf *et al.* argue: 'The entire basis of this study rests on the unassailable assumption that we can tell something about the future by looking at the past...[but] why might the future look nothing at all like the past?' (Wolf *et al.* 2003:48). Thus, even though 'water wars' may be a myth, the relationship between political stability and water is certainly not (Wolf 1998) and future water wars may still be a reality. 'In principle conflicts might escalate due to the incapacity of local and traditional authorities to regulate growing tensions; [or] due to lack of policies to deal with such issues on a national level; or due to a low level of regional cooperation' (Ludi 2002:23). Nevertheless, 'If there is to be water related violence in the future, it is much more liable to be like "water riots" ... than "water wars" across national boundaries' (Wolf *et al.* 2003:50).

The fall of the Mubarak regime and 'water riots'
The Arab Spring of 2011 that led to the fall of several Arab regimes in the Middle East was generally portrayed in the media as a fight for democracy against autocrats, tyrants or dictators. The surge towards democracy was of course a crucial driver, but behind this there was another consideration, spiking food prices.

In Tunisia the uprising began as a protest over the price of bread. In Cairo, demonstrators initially chanted 'Bread and freedom!' Although the uprisings were not ultimately about food, increasing prices became catalysts for greater tensions.[30] This has a parallel with the uprisings in Egypt of 1977, when government tried to rescind food subsidises. As Waterbury (1983:230) has noted, 'it has become a given of Egyptian politics that the bread subsidy cannot be touched except at the peril of the regime.' Other rulers in the Middle East have also learned this lesson: plenty of cheap government-subsidised food secures stability. However, these subsidies came at a high cost – unemployment – because the agricultural sector became hollowed out, leading to instability. When prices of grain began skyrocketing in 2008, 'democracies of bread' riots broke out in Jordan, Morocco, Algeria, Lebanon, Syria and Yemen. From February 2007 to February 2008, bread prices in Egypt arose by 37 per cent and people died on Egypt's bread lines. There was public outrage over these 'bread martyrs', but prices went from bad to worse, reaching an all-time high in early 2011.[31]

Although the Arab Spring is not reducible to a single factor, in regard to 'virtual water' and its impact on 'water wars', Egypt may prove to be an example, since the country is the world's biggest importer of wheat. Decreases in water availability and subsequent food production may spark tensions and uprisings. Egypt's management of water and agricultural production of non-food crops such as cotton may intensify such conflicts and autocratic regimes may fall through their own water policies. Moreover, and perhaps more importantly, with regard to 'virtual water' and Egypt, food imports cannot guarantee food security if the country's population has not enough money to buy them. The Arab Spring helps to underscore the extreme vulnerability of an approach that is tied to volatile global market prices which directly impact people's lives and wellbeing, even where food is heavily subsidised. Accessing 'virtual water' food is a sub-optimal option for poor people: a last option in the short run, but not a viable solution in the long term.

Other 'water riots' are possibly also on the horizon, as are different policies aimed at avoiding such conflicts over water resources or the impact of changing habitats on livelihoods. Egypt and Sudan remain strong advocates of the Jonglei Canal, since it will enhance the amount of water available to downstream users. South Sudan may also benefit from this water in future irrigation projects. Despite this, the project remains taboo among officials in South Sudan because it will greatly alter the way of living among the Nilotic tribes in the Sudd, who depend on the seasonal variations for their pastoral economies. There is a fear

---

30. http://www.theglobeandmail.com/news/opinions/opinion/the-dangers-of-treating-food-as-a-strategic-asset/article1886971/ (accessed 5 March 2012).
31. http://www.foreignaffairs.com/articles/67672/annia-ciezadlo/let-them-eat-bread (accessed 5 March 2012).

that this may lead to a new civil war, the last thing the newly independent South Sudan needs in its difficult start as a young nation.[32]

Thus, 'water riots' and 'water wars' within and among states may take place in the future, or water may be a source of cooperation within and across nations. Given increasing population, more stress on water and land resources and the possibly severe effects of climate change, how struggles over water will be resolved in future remains highly uncertain.

---

32. Châtel, F. and T. Oestigaard (2012), 'The Nile: Shifting Balance of Powers', *Revolve*: 32–9.

What chiefly characterises the future of the Nile is the uncertainties associated with coming challenges. These uncertainties have formed part of the negotiations in the Nile Basin and the Cooperative Framework Agreement has changed the premises for utilisation of the Nile in the decades to come. Nevertheless, what can be predicted in this uncertain world is that in the future the premises and challenges will change again. Adding to this, different researchers and politicians may choose to evaluate and emphasise the importance of factors and actors in different ways, and these differences may ultimately have political implications and consequences. Moreover, although I have done my best to refer to current data and analyses (which often differ), there are many uncertainties and differing estimates underpinning the divergent scenarios. Such uncertainties and unknowns have also to be incorporated into today's and tomorrow's political planning and implementation. This is, of course, in practice virtually impossible and relates directly to the overall question I have aimed to discuss:

Will there be enough water in the Nile Basin for food production so that the basin as a whole or individual countries will achieve food security in the future?

As shown, this is a difficult question to answer conclusively for a number of reasons, because there might be more water. First, throughout the basin it is possible to save more water by reassessing crop choices, modernising irrigation methods, treating wastewater, improving urban networks and reducing leakages from pipes. Vast amounts of water are also wasted through evaporation in many dams. Moreover, Egypt has been accused of pumping water out of the basin to irrigation projects in the Sinai and the New Valley projects – both located in extremely hot deserts. Thus, it is possible to increase the overall water availability by improving water management practices throughout the basin.

Second, 'societies along the Nile are neither equally capable of harming their common resource nor equally likely to suffer the consequences of others' behaviour, not only because some live upstream and others downstream, but also because individual action need not negatively affect other actors (although this of course may happen, and very deliberately so)' (Tvedt 2010d:240). In particular, Egypt may benefit from hydroelectric dams upstream. Although more dams in Ethiopia (and Sudan) may temporarily reduce the flow of the Nile in Egypt, hydropower dams will not function unless the water is released and thus will flow downstream. Consequently, hydropower projects are not a major threat to overall water supply and availability in the Nile Basin. Importantly, the Blue Nile carries enormous loads of silt, which will ultimately fill the Aswan Dam and cause its destruction. More dams upstream catching this silt will prolong the life of the Aswan Dam. Moreover, in a basin-wide perspective, storing water in the Grand Renaissance Dam in Ethiopia may also benefit Egypt since about 10 bcm of water evaporates annually from Lake Nasser. If the water is stored in a cooler climate in Ethiopia during the hottest summer months in Egypt, and released during the more favourable winter months, it may be possible to reduce evaporation in Lake Nasser by 3–5 bcm or more, thereby increasing the overall amount of water in Egypt.[33] This, however, implies that control of Egypt's water security lies beyond the country's borders, a circumstance at odds with the policy behind the building of the Aswan Dam.

Third, there are many uncertainties about the Nubian sandstone aquifer in the eastern Sahara (Egypt, northern Sudan and eastern Libya). Since the beginning of the 19th century, the aquifer has been the subject of hundreds of studies. Estimates have shown that total groundwater storage is about 135,000 km^3 (Gossel, Ebraheem and Wycisk 2004) or in the range of 150,000 km^3 (Faure, Walter and Grant 2002) and even higher. However, there is less clarity about the actual potential of this reservoir. Another potential source of water expansion is desalination of water from the Mediterranean. Finally, if the Jonglei Canal is completed, it will also increase the flows in the Nile.

Thus, there may be more water in the Nile Basin in the future, but this is uncertain. Adding to this uncertainty is climate change, which may or may not make of the basin a drier regime. What seems beyond doubt is that rapid population growth will continue. Even if the hydrological parameters of the Nile Basin do not change and the amount of water remains the same as today (which may or may not be likely), the prospects of their being enough water in the Nile Basin for future food security are not very promising. Today, the current populations of Nile Basin countries are haunted by poverty and unable to achieve food security. How it will be possible to have food security for populations twice or thrice as large seems difficult to forecast, given that all indexes and predictions suggest there will be more stress and pressure on each drop of water.

'Good governance' is often heralded as the solution to development and utilisation of water, land and human resources in a region with plenty of resources, albeit unevenly distributed. Juma has argued in *The New Harvest. Agricultural Innovation in Africa* (2011) that Africa has the potential to be food self-sufficient and more with good governance and technological innovation. One cannot disagree with his positive view of the potential, but there are, however, perhaps serious obstacles to the realisation of his vision of entrepreneurial leadership dedicated to economic improvement. One is that for this to happen, water must be given a top priority on the political agenda.

In current global discourse, there is strong emphasis on recognising water in global policy. Water enjoys high priority within the UN and forums such as the G8/G20, the World Economic Forum and the World Water Forum. All of them emphasise

33. http://newbusinessethiopia.com/index.php?option=com_contentandview=articleandid=46 3:ethiopia-vow-to-fully-finance-millennium-dam-on-nile-river-andcatid=38:governmentan dItemid=38 (accessed 6 March 2012).

water's fundamental role in socioeconomic development. But, and herein lies perhaps both the core problem and the solution, 'although these processes [and organisations] can have a significant influence on national policy, their agendas and negotiations are in fact driven by the member states. It is therefore up to the different member states themselves to take leadership and ensure that water is put on the agenda of these processes' (UN Water 2012:35). This will also address the question of food security.

In other words, global discourse on water footprints, worldwide food production, virtual water and food imports in water-scarce areas has little practical relevance to individual nation states. One may interpret the preceding quotation to mean that global water policy and hence food security policy may be difficult to achieve. This partly relates to the 'virtual water' discussions, because poor nations cannot base their food security on today's global market: without production systems that generate income it is impossible to buy food. Free food in the form of development aid is hardly an option for sustainable development. Thus, developing food and water security systems is first and foremost a national responsibility, and this represents huge challenges for Nile Basin countries.

However, as I have aimed to show, the premises for today's policies are rooted in part in past colonial policies. These include previous agreements for sharing the Nile's water, huge irrigation schemes like the Gezira and water-intensive cotton production systems in Egypt. Importantly, water structures such as dams and irrigation schemes are long lasting and impact future water policies. Thus, the 'right' policy at one time may be a hindrance or problem at another. British cotton production is an example. The Aswan High Dam may also be seen as a double edged sword. On the one hand, it has secured to Egypt stable water resources for both energy and agriculture and has enabled Egypt to develop. On the other hand, evaporation from Lake Nasser reduces the overall water in the Nile significantly. Moreover, when the dam eventually silts up, Egypt will face new problems of an unprecedented scale. The different climate change scenarios also pose challenges for making the right decisions. If there will actually be more water in the first half of this century and less in the second, how is it possible to develop water structures that take into account both outcomes?

Currently, building dams seems to be the only practical and realistic solution, which also increases the energy security of the respective countries. However, all the planned irrigation schemes in the basin will require substantially more water than currently flows in the Nile. Improved irrigation efficiency may save water in the sense that there will be 'more crops per drop', but given estimated population increase it seems unrealistic that improved irrigation will reduce overall water consumption in irrigated agriculture in the basin as a whole. Moreover, most of the people in the Nile Basin will still depend on rainfed agriculture for subsistence and, as such, the future potential of irrigation is limited. This draws our attention to the types of crops being cultivated.

The recent trend has been that more and more land is not used for food production but for growing cash crops that generate a (relatively) high income. This is an understandable policy in the short run, but may prove detrimental to food security in the longer run, given that famine regularly haunts many of the Nile Basin countries today. How much of the money from foreign direct investments actually remains in the receiving countries and is used for agricultural or other development purposes is another question. As with the building of dams and construction of cotton irrigation schemes in the early 20th century, the policy of leasing out land for biofuel production will have profound implications for future agriculture. Many of the contracts have a term of 99 years and the food production potential of these areas may therefore be sealed for the next century.

Agriculture in Africa, as elsewhere, is intrinsically interwoven into the global economy. Food security in the form of 'virtual water' imports will hardly be a viable option, basically because this option requires an economic surplus which most sub-Saharan farmers depending on rainfed agriculture are unlikely to achieve. With increasing population growth, there will an ever increasing need for water for food production. It is uncertain that there will be enough water, since overall food security is already jeopardised or under high water threat and stress. According to the Cooperative Framework Agreement, the Nile water resources will be shared 'in an equitable and reasonable manner' following 'the principle of preventing the causing of significant harm to other States of the Nile River Basin'. How this will be achieved in practice is highly uncertain, since agriculture is the main consumer of water and is in increasing competition with industrial and urban consumers. Thus, one may fear there will be insufficient water for everyone. Ultimately, then, the Nile issue is a matter of life and death.

These are the stakes Nile Basin states face and have to incorporate in their policy planning and implementation. This is the situation today and the challenges will be more fundamental tomorrow and in the future. At the same time, transboundary river management in a catchment area like the Nile Basin is so complex and involves so many uncertainties and sometimes competing interests within and among nation states that it is difficult, if not impossible, to have a full grasp of the factual premises today, let alone tomorrow's changed scenarios and issues – in other words, to know what the right political decisions should be, yet decisions will have to be made. As a consequence, with increased population and higher stress on water resources and food security, there might be both more tension and conflict as well as cooperation in different places and at different times. The ways in which the Nile issues are resolved, or not, may also serve as lessons for other transboundary rivers. The Nile will therefore be of global concern and interest in decades to come, and the question of water for food production and food security will have ever greater importance in the future.

References

Adar, K.G. (2011), 'Kenya's foreign-policy and geoploitical interests: The case of the Nile River Basin', in K.G. Adar and N.A. Check (eds), *Cooperative Diplomacy, Regional Stability and National Interests. The Nile River and the Riparian States*, Africa Institute of South Africa, Pretoria: 167–88.

Alemayehu, T., M. McCartney and S. Kebede (2010), 'The water resource implications of planned development in the Lake Tana catchment, Ethiopia', *Ecohydrology and Hydrobiology*, Vol. 10, No. 2–4: 211–22.

Allen, J.A. (1996), 'Policy responses to the closure of water resources', in P. Howsam and R. Carter (eds), *Water Policy: Allocation and Management in Practice*, Chapman and Hall, London.

Allen, J.A. (1998), 'Virtual Water: A Strategic Resource. Global Solutions to Regional Deficits', *Ground Water*, Vol. 36, No. 4: 545–6.

Allen, J.A. (2002), 'Hydro-Peace in the Middle East: Why no Water Wars? A Case Study of the Jordan River Basin', *SAIS Review*, Vol. XXII, No. 2: 255–72.

Allan, J.A. (2003), 'Virtual Water – the Water, Food, and Trade Nexus. Useful Concepts or Misleading Metaphor?', *International Water*, Vol. 28, No. 1: 4–11.

Anseeuw, W. *et al.* (2012), *Land Rights and the Rush for Land. Findings of the Global Commercial Pressures on Land Research Project*, ILC, Rome.

Arsano, Y. (2007), *Ethiopia and the Nile. Dilemmas of National and Regional Hydropolitics*, ETH, Zurich.

Arsano, Y. (2010), 'Institutional Development and Water Management in the Ethiopian Nile Basin', in T. Tvedt (ed.), *The River Nile in the Post-Colonial Age*, I.B. Tauris, London: 161–78.

Awulachew, S., L-M.Rebelo and D. Molden (2010), 'The Nile Basin: Tapping the unmet agricultural potential of Nile waters', *Water International*, Vol. 35, No. 5: 623–54.

Awulachew, S. and M. Ayana (2011), 'Performance of irrigation: An assessment at different scales in Ethiopia', *Expl Agric.*, Vol. 47: 57–69.

Benedick, R.E. (1979), 'The High Dam and the transformation of the Nile', *Middle East Journal*, Vol. 33, No. 2: 119–44.

Beyene, A. (2011), 'Smallholder-led transformation towards biofuel production in Ethiopia', in P.B. Matondi, K. Havnevik and A. Beyene (eds), *Biofuls, land grabbing and food security in Africa*, Zed Books, London: 90–105.

Boserup, E. (1965), *The Conditions of Agricultural Growth: The Economics of Agrarian Change Under Population Pressure*, Allen and Unwin, London.

Brown, A. and M.D. Matlock (2011), 'A Review of Water Scarcity Indices and Methodologies', Sustainability Consortium White Paper 106, http://www.sustainabilityconsortium.org/wp-content/themes/sustainability/assets/pdf/whitepapers/2011_Brown_Matlock_Water-Availability-Assessment-Indices-and-Methodologies-Lit-Review.pdf (accessed 26 February 2012).

Bohle, H.G. (2001), 'Food Security', in *International Encyclopedia of the Social and Behavioral Sciences*: 5728–30.

Bosire, R.M. (2011), 'Tanzania: Multilateralism and national interests in the Nile River Basin question' , in K.G. Adar and N.A. Check (eds), *Cooperative Diplomacy, Regional Stability and National Interests. The Nile River and the Riparian States*, Africa Institute of South Africa, Pretoria: 189–214.

Bushara, A.I. and T. Abdelrahim (2010), 'Investigation of Step Trends of the Nile River Flow Time Series', *Nile Basin Water Science and Engineering Journal*, Vol. 3, Issue 2: 15–24.

Carius, A., G.A. Dabelko and A. Wolf (2004), 'Water, Conflict, and Cooperation', *ECSP REPORT*, Issue 10 (2004): 60–6.

Cascão, A.E. (2009), 'Changing Power Relations in the Nile River Basin: Unilateralism vs. Cooperation?., *Water Alternatives*, Vol. 2, No. 2: 245–68.

Castillo, G.E., R.E. Namara *et al.* (2007), 'Reversing the flow: Agricultural water management pathways for poverty reduction', in D. Molden (ed.), *Water for food, water for life: a comprehensive assessment of water management in agriculture*, International Water Management Institute, Colombo and Earthscan, London: 149–91.

CGAAER (2012), *Water and Food Security facing Global Challenges: What Challenges, What Solutions?* CGAAER, Paris.

Chapagain, A.K. *et al.* (2005), 'The Water Footprint of Cotton Consumption', *Value of Water* Research Report Series No. 18, UNESCO-IHE, Delft.

Churchill, W. (1933). *The River War*, Eyre and Spottiswoode, London.

Cook, S., M. Fisher, T. Tiemann and A. Vidal (2011), 'Water, food and poverty: Global- and basin-scale analysis', *Water International*, Vol. 26, No. 1: 1–16.

Darby, L., P. Ghalioungui and L. Grivetti (1977a), *Food: The Gift of Osiris, Volume 1*, Academic Press, London.

Deng, B.K. (2011), 'Cooperation between Egypt and Sudan over the Nile River waters: The challenges of duality', in K.G. Adar and N.A. Check (eds), *Cooperative Diplomacy, Regional Stability and National Interests. The Nile River and the Riparian States*, Africa Institute of South Africa, Pretoria: 39–66.

Elemam, H.E.R. (2010), 'Egypt and Collective Action Mechanisms in the Nile Basin', in T. Tvedt (ed.), *The River Nile in the Post-Colonial Age*, I.B. Tauris, London: 217–36.

Elshamy, M.E. *et al.* (2009), 'Impacts of climate change on the Nile Flows at Dongola Using Statistical Downscaled GCM Scenarios', *Nile Basin Water Science and Engineering Journal*, Vol. 3, Issue 2: 114.

Elshamy, M.E., I.A. Seierstad and A. Sorteberg (2008), 'Impacts of climate change on Blue Nile flows using bias-corrected GCM scenarios', *Hydrology and Earth System Sciences Discussions*, Vol. 5: 1407–39.

Falkenmark, M. (1989), 'The massive water scarcity threatening Africa – why isn't being addressed?' *Ambio*, Vol. 2: 112–18.

FAO (1996), *Report of the World Food Summit*, FAO, Rome.

FAO (2005), *Irrigation in Africa in figures. AQUASTAT Survey 2005*, FAO, Rome.

Faure, H., R.C.Walter and D.R. Grant (2002), 'The coastal oasis: Ice age springs on emerged continental shelves', *Global and Planetary Change*, Vol. 33, Issues 1–2, June:47–56.

Faurès, J-M. *et al.* (2007), 'Reinventing irrigation', in D. Molden (ed.), *Water for food, water for life: a comprehensive assessment of water management in agriculture*, International Water Management Institute, Colombo and Earthscan, London: 353–94.

Food Outlook (2010), *Food Outlook. Global Market Analysis June 2010*, FAO, Rome.

Food Price Watch (2011a), *Food Price Watch April 2011*, World Bank, Washington DC.

Food Price Watch (2011b), *Food Price Watch August 2011*, World Bank Washington DC.

Food Price Watch (2011c), *Food Price Watch November 2011*, World Bank Washington DC.

Fraiture, C. *et al.* (2004), *Comprehensive Assessment Research Report 4. Does International Cereal Trade Save Water? The Impact of Virtual Water Trade on Global Water Use*, International Water Management Institute, Colombo.

Fraiture, C. and D. Wichelens (2007), 'Looking ahead to 2050: scenarios of alternative investment approaches', in D. Molden (ed.), *Water for food, water for life: A comprehensive assessment of water management in agriculture*, International Water Management Institute, Colombo and Earthscan, London: 91–145.

Fraiture, C. and D. Wichelens (2010), 'Satisfying future water demands for agriculture', *Agricultural Water Management*, Vol. 97: 502–11.

Fraiture, C., D. Molden and D.Wichelens (2010), 'Investing in water for food, ecosystems, and livelihoods: An overview of the comprehensive assessment of water management in agriculture', *Agriculture Water Management*, Vol. 97: 495–501.

Fresco, L.O. (2009), 'Challenges for food system adaptation today and tomorrow', *Environmental Science and Policy*, Vol. 2: 378–85.

Gerbens-Leenes, W. and A.Y. Hoekstra, (2011), 'The water footprint of biofuel-based transport', *Energy and Environmental Science*, Vol. 4: 2658–68.

Gohar, A.A. and F.A. Ward (2011), 'Gains from Improved Irrigation Water Use Efficiency in Egypt', *International Journal of Water Resource Development*, Vol. 27, No. 4: 737–58.

Gossel, W., A.M. Ebraheem and P. Wycisk (2004), 'A very large scale GIS-based groundwater flow model for the Nubian sandstone aquifer in Eastern Sahara (Egypt, northern Sudan and eastern Libya)', *Hydrogeology Journal*, Vol. 12: 698–713.

Government of Sudan and the World Bank (2000), *Sudan. Options for the Sustainable Development of the Gezira Scheme*.

Grain (2012), *Squeezing Africa Dry: Behind every land grab is a water grab*. Grain report June 2012. Grain. Barcelona.

Granit, J. *et al.* (2010), *Regional Water Intelligence Report. The Nile Basin and the Southern Sudan Referendum,* SIWI Paper 18, Stockholm International Water Institute, Stockholm.

Hagos, F. *et al.* (2009), *Importance of irrigated Agriculture to the Ethiopia Economy: Capturing the Direct Net Benefits of irrigation,* IWMI research Report 128, International Water Management Institute, Colombo.

Hanjra, M.A. and M.E. Quereshi (2010), 'Global water crisis and future food security in an era of climate change', *Food Policy,* Vol. 35: 365–77.

Hassan, H.A. and A.A. Rasheedy (2011), 'The Nile River and Egyptian foreign-policy interests', in K.G. Adar and N.A. Check (eds), *Cooperative Diplomacy, Regional Stability and National Interests. The Nile River and the Riparian States,* Africa Institute of South Africa, Pretoria: 131–52.

Havnevik, K. (2011), 'Grabbing of African lands for energy and food: Implications for land rights, food security and smallholders', in P.B. Matondi, K. Havnevik and A. Beyene (eds), *Biofuels, land grabbing and food security in Africa,* Zed Books, London: 20–43.

Himdan, J. (1987), *The character of Egypt,* Alam Al Kotob, Cairo.

Hultin, J. (1995), 'The Nile: Source of life, source of conflict', in L. Ohlsson (ed.), *Hydropolitics: Conflicts over water as a development constraint,* Zed Books, London.

Human Development Report (2011), *Sustainability and Equity: A Better Future for All,* UNDP, New York.

Hårsmar, M. (2010), Why is agriculture so important to reducing poverty? *NAI Policy Note 7(2010).* The Nordic Africa Institute. Uppsala.

Inocencio, A. *et al.* (2007), *Research Report 109. Costs and Performance of Irrigation Projects: A Comparison of sub-Saharan Africa and Other Developing Regions,* International Water Management Institute, Colombo.

IPCC (Intergovernmental Panel on Climate Change) (2007), Annex II: Glossary of synthesis report, A.P.M. Baede (ed.), *IPCC Fourth Assessment Report: Climate Change 2007: Synthesis Report,* Geneva, IPCC, www.ipcc.ch/pdf/assessment-report/ar4/syr/ar4_syr_appendix.pdf (accessed 19 March 2012).

Joesten, J. (1960), 'Nasser's Daring Dream: The Aswan High Dam', *World Today,* Vol. 16, No. 2: 55–63.

Jonglei Investigation Team (1953), 'The Equatorial Nile Project and Its Effects in Sudan', *Geographical Journal,* Vol. 119: 33–48.

Juma, C. (2011), *The New Harvest: Agricultural Innovation in Africa,* Oxford University Press, Oxford.

Jägerskog, A. and M. Zeitoun (2009). *Getting Transboundary Water Right: Theory and Practice for Effective Cooperation.* Report Nr. 25. Stockholm, SIWI.

Jägerskog, A., A. Cascao, M. Hårsmar and K. Kim (2012), *Land Acquisitions: How Will they Impact Trandboundary Waters,* SIWI Report 30, *SIWI,* Stockholm.

Kassa, T. (2010), 'International Law and Moderations of Physical Geography: The Nile Setting', in T. Tvedt, G. Chapman and R. Hagen (eds), *A History of Water Series II, Volume 3. Water, Geopolitics and the new World Order,* I.B. Tauris, London: 472–94.

Kazimbazi, E.B. (2010), 'The impact of colonial agreements on the regulation of the waters of the River Nile', *Water International,* Vol. 35, No. 6: 718–32.

Keller, A. and J. Keller (1995), *Effective Efficiency: A Water Use Efficiency Concept for Allocating Fresh Water Resources,* Discussion Paper 22, Center for Economic Policy Studies, Princeton.

Keller, J., A. Keller and G. Davids (1998), 'River basin development phases and implications of closure', *Journal of Applied Irrigation Science,* Vol. 33, No. 2: 145–63.

Kim, U. *et al.* (2008), *Climate Change Impacts on Hydrology and Water Resources of the Upper Blue Nile River Basin, Ethiopia,* International Water Management Institute Research Report 126, International Water Management Institute Research, Colombo.

Langer, W.L. (1936), 'The Struggle for the Nile', *Foreign Affairs,* Vol. 14, No. 2: 259–73.

Lawrence, P., J. Meigh and C. Sullivan (2002), 'The Water Poverty Index: An international Comparison', *Keele Economics Research Papers* 2002/19, Keele University, Staffordshire.

Ludi, E. (2002), 'Household and Communal Strategies Dealing with Degradation of and Conflicts Over Natural Resources: Case Studies from the Ethiopian Highlands', in G. Baechler, K. Spillmann and M. Suliman (eds), *Transformation of Resource Conflict: Approach and Instrument,* Peter Lang, London.

Malthus, T.R. (1798), *An Essay on the Principle of population, As It Affects the Future Improvement of Society,* John Murray, London.

Matondi, P.B., K. Havnevik and A. Beyene (2011a), 'Introduction: Biofuels, food security and land grabbing in Africa', in P.B. Matondi, K. Havnevik and A. Beyene (eds), *Biofuels, land grabbing and food security in Africa,* Zed Books, London:1–19.

Matondi, P.B., K. Havnevik and A. Beyene, A. (2011b), 'Conclusion: Land grabbing, smallholder farmers and the meaning of agro-investor-driven agrarian change in Africa', in P.B. Matondi, K. Havnevik and A. Beyene (eds), *Biofuels, land grabbing and food security in Africa,* Zed Books, London.

McCartney, M. *et al.* (2010), *Evaluation of Current and Future Water Resources Development in the Lake Tana Basin, Ethiopia,* Project Number 59, Challenge Programme on Water and Food, International Water Management Institute, Colombo.

Mehta, L. *et al.* (2012), 'Introduction to the Special Issue: Water Grabbing? Focus on the (Re)appropriation of Finite Water Resources', *Water Alternatives,* 5(2): 193–207.

Millennium Development Goals Report (2011), United Nations, New York.

Mohammed, Y.A. *et al.* (2005), 'New lessons of the Sudd hydrology learned from remote sensing and climate modeling', *Hydrology and Earth System Sciences Discussions*, Vol. 2: 1503–35.

Molden, D. *et al.* (2007), 'Trends in water and agricultural development', in D. Molden (ed.), *Water for food, water for life: A comprehensive assessment of water management in agriculture,* International Water Management Institute, Colombo and Earthscan, London:57–89.

Molden, D., S.B.Awulachew, K.Conniff *et al.* (2009), *Nile Basin Focal Project. Synthesis Report,* Project Number 59, Challenge Programme on Water and Food, International Water Management Institute, Colombo.

Nile Basin Initiative (2012), *OneRiver One People OneVision*, NBI, Entebbe.

Oakland Institute (2011), *Understanding land investment deals in Africa. Country Report: Ethiopi,* Oakland Institute, Oakland.

Oestigaard, T. (2009), 'Water, Culture and Identity. Comparing Past and Present Traditions in the Nile Basin Region', in T. Oestigaard (ed.), *Water, Culture and Identity. Comparing Past and Present Traditions in the Nile Basin Region,* BRIC Press, Bergen: 11–22.

Oestigaard, T. (2011a), *Water and climate change in Africa – from causes to consequences,* NAI Policy Note 4, Nordic Africa Institute, Uppsala.

Oestigaard, T. (2011b), *Horus' Eye and Osiris' Efflux: The Egyptian Civilization of Inundation ca.3000–2000 BCE,* Archaeopress, Oxford.

Oestigaard, T. (2012), 'When everything depends on the rain: Drought, rain-fed agriculture and food security', *Nordic Africa Institute Annual Report (2010),* Nordic Africa Institute, Uppsala.

Oestigaard, T. (in prep.), *Globalized traditions. Rainmaking, witchcraft and Christianity in Tanzania.*

Ravnborg, H.M. (2004), 'Introduction: From Water "Wars" to Water "Riots"?', in J. Boesen H.M. Ravnborg (eds), *From Water 'Wars' to Water 'Riots'? Lessons from Transboundary Water Management,* Proceedings of the International Conference, December 2003, DIIS, Copenhagen.

Rockström, J. *et al.* (2007), 'Managing water in rainfed agriculture', in D. Molden (ed.), *Water for food, water for life: A comprehensive assessment of water management in agriculture,* International Water Management Institute, Colombo and Earthscan, London, pp. 315–52.

Rosegrant, M.W., C. Ringler and T. Zhu (2009), 'Water for Agriculture: Maintaining Food Security under Growing Scarcity', *Annual Review of Environment and Resources,* Vol. 34: 205–22.

Salman, S.M.A. (2011), 'The new state of South Sudan and the hydro-politics of the Nile Basin', *Water International*, Vol. 36, No. 2, 154–66.

Shippers, J.C. (2012), 'How desalination works', *Revolve Water Around the Mediterranean*: 82–4.

Schnitter, N.J. (1994), *A History of Dams. The Useful Pyramids*, A.A.Balkema, Rotterdam.

Taha, F. (2010), 'The History of Nile Waters in the Sudan', in T. Tvedt (ed.), *The River Nile in the Post-Colonial Age*, I.B. Tauris, London: 179–216.

Tvedt, T. (2004), *The River Nile in the Age of the British. Political Ecology and the Quest for Economic Power*, I.B. Tauris, London.

Tvedt, T. (2010a), 'Why England and not China and India? Water systems and the history of the industrial revolution', *Journal of Global History*, Vol. 5: 29–50.

Tvedt, T. (2010b), 'Bridging the Gap: A Water System Approach', in W. Østreng (ed.), *Transference. Interdisciplinary Communications 2008/2009*, Centre for Advanced Study, Oslo, http://www.cas.uio.no/Publications/Seminar/0809Tvedt.pdf

Tvedt, T. (2010c), 'Water: A Source of Wars or a Pathway to Peace? An Empirical Critique of Two Dominant Schools of Thought on Water and International Politics', in T. Tvedt, G. Chapman and R. Hagen (eds), *A History of Water Series II, Volume 3. Water, Geopolitics and the new World Order*, I.B. Tauris, London: 78–108.

Tvedt, T. (2010d), 'Some Conceptual Issues Regarding the Study of Inter-state Relationships in River Basins', in T. Tvedt (ed.), *The River Nile in the Post-Colonial Age*, I.B. Tauris, London: 237–46.

Tvedt, T. and R. Coopey (eds), (2010), *A History of Water. Series 2, Vol. 2. Rivers and Society: From Early Civilizations to Modern Times*, I.B. Tauris, London.

Toulmin, C. (2010), *Climate Change in Africa. African Arguments*, Zed Books, London.

United Nations Economic Commission for Africa, African Climate Policy Center (2011), *Agricultural Water Management in the Context of Climate Change in Africa*, Working Paper 9, Addis Ababa.

UN Water (2007), *Coping with water scarcity. Challenge of the twenty-first century*, FAO, Rome.

UN Water (2009), *The United Nations World Water Development Report 3. Water in a changing world*, UNESCO, Paris.

UN Water (2012), *Managing Water under Uncertainty and Risk. The United Nations World water Development Report 4*, UNESCO, Paris.

UN (2009), *World population prospects: The 2008 revision* [online]. Population Newsletter 87, June, New York, Population Division of the Department of Economic and Social Affairs of the United Nations (UN) Secretariat, http://www.un.org/esa/population/publications/wpp2008/wpp2008_text_tables.pdf (accessed 9 January 2012).

Vermeulen, S.L. *et al.* (2012), 'Options for support to agriculture and food security under climate change', *Environmental Science and Policy*, Vol. 15: 136–44.

Waterbury, J. (1979), *Hydropolitics of the Nile Valley*, Syracuse University Press, New York.

Waterbury, J. (1983), *The Egypt of Nasser and Sadat. The Political Economy of Two Regimes*, Princeton University Press, New Jersey.

Wichelns, D. (2010), 'Virtual Water and Water Footprints Offer Limited Insight Regarding Imp ortant Policy Questions', *International Journal of Water Resources Development*, Vol. 26, No. 4: 639–51.

Wild, R.A. (1981), *Water in the Cultic Worship of Isis and Sarapis*, Brill, Leiden.

Wolf, A. (1998), 'Conflict and cooperation along international waterways', *Water Policy* Vol. 1, No. 2: 251–65.

Wolf, A. *et al.* (2003), 'International waters: Identifying basins at risk', *Water Policy* Vol. 5: 29–60.

World Bank (1986), *Poverty and Hunger*, World Bank, Washington, DC.

World Bank (2007), *MENA Develop Report. Making the Most of Scarcity. Accountability for Better Water Management in the Middle East and North Africa*, World Bank, Washington, DC.

World Food Council (1988), *Towards Sustainable Food Security: Critical Issues*, Report by the Secretariat, 14th Ministerial Session, Nicosia, Cyprus, 23–26 May.

Yacob, Y. (2004), 'From UNDUGU to the Nile Basin Initiative: An Enduring Exercise in Futility', *Addis Tribune*, 30 January 2004.

CURRENT AFRICAN ISSUES PUBLISHED BY THE INSTITUTE

Recent issues in the series are available electronically
for download free of charge www.nai.uu.se

1. *South Africa, the West and the Frontline States. Report from a Seminar.* 1981, 34 pp, (out-of print)

2. Maja Naur, *Social and Organisational Change in Libya.* 1982, 33 pp, (out-of print)

3. *Peasants and Agricultural Production in Africa. A Nordic Research Seminar. Follow-up Reports and Discussions.* 1981, 34 pp, (out-of print)

4. Ray Bush & S. Kibble, *Destabilisation in Southern Africa, an Overview.* 1985, 48 pp, (out-of print)

5. Bertil Egerö, *Mozambique and the Southern African Struggle for Liberation.* 1985, 29 pp, (out-of print)

6. Carol B.Thompson, *Regional Economic Polic under Crisis Condition. Southern African Development.* 1986, 34 pp, (out-of print)

7. Inge Tvedten, *The War in Angola, Internal Conditions for Peace and Recovery.* 1989, 14 pp, (out-of print)

8. Patrick Wilmot, *Nigeria's Southern Africa Policy 1960–1988.* 1989, 15 pp, (out-of print)

9. Jonathan Baker, *Perestroika for Ethiopia: In Search of the End of the Rainbow?* 1990, 21 pp, (out-of print)

10. Horace Campbell, *The Siege of Cuito Cuanavale.* 1990, 35 pp, (out-of print)

11. Maria Bongartz, *The Civil War in Somalia. Its genesis and dynamics.* 1991, 26 pp, (out-of print)

12. Shadrack B.O. Gutto, *Human and People's Rights in Africa. Myths, Realities and Prospects.* 1991, 26 pp, (out-of print)

13. Said Chikhi, Algeria. *From Mass Rebellion to Workers' Protest.* 1991, 23 pp, (out-of print)

14. Bertil Odén, *Namibia's Economic Links to South Africa.* 1991, 43 pp, (out-of print)

15. Cervenka Zdenek, *African National Congress Meets Eastern Europe. A Dialogue on Common Experiences.* 1992, 49 pp, ISBN 91-7106-337-4, (out-of print)

16. Diallo Garba, *Mauritania–The Other Apartheid?* 1993, 75 pp, ISBN 91-7106-339-0, (out-of print)

17. Zdenek Cervenka and Colin Legum, *Can National Dialogue Break the Power of Terror in Burundi?* 1994, 30 pp, ISBN 91-7106-353-6, (out-of print)

18. Erik Nordberg and Uno Winblad, *Urban Environmental Health and Hygiene in Sub- Saharan Africa.* 1994, 26 pp, ISBN 91-7106-364-1, (out-of print)

19. Chris Dunton and Mai Palmberg, *Human Rights and Homosexuality in Southern Africa.* 1996, 48 pp, ISBN 91-7106-402-8, (out-of print)

20. Georges Nzongola-Ntalaja *From Zaire to the Democratic Republic of the Congo.* 1998, 18 pp, ISBN 91-7106-424-9, (out-of print)

21. Filip Reyntjens, *Talking or Fighting? Political Evolution in Rwanda and Burundi, 1998–1999.* 1999, 27 pp, ISBN 91-7106-454-0, SEK 80.-

22. Herbert Weiss, *War and Peace in the Democratic Republic of the Congo.* 1999, 28 pp, ISBN 91-7106-458-3, SEK 80,-

23. Filip Reyntjens, *Small States in an Unstable Region – Rwanda and Burundi, 1999–2000,* 2000, 24 pp, ISBN 91-7106-463-X, (out-of print)

24. Filip Reyntjens, *Again at the Crossroads: Rwanda and Burundi, 2000–2001.* 2001, 25 pp, ISBN 91-7106-483-4, (out-of print)

25. Henning Melber, *The New African Initiative and the African Union. A Preliminary Assessment and Documentation.* 2001, 36 pp, ISBN 91-7106-486-9, (out-of print)

26. Dahilon Yassin Mohamoda, *Nile Basin Cooperation. A Review of the Literature.* 2003, 39 pp, ISBN 91-7106-512-1, SEK 90,-

27. Henning Melber (ed.), *Media, Public Discourse and Political Contestation in Zimbabwe.* 2004, 39 pp, ISBN 91-7106-534-2, SEK 90,-

28. Georges Nzongola-Ntalaja, *From Zaire to the Democratic Republic of the Congo. Second and Revised Edition.* 2004, 23 pp, ISBN-91-7106-538-5, (out-of print)

29. Henning Melber (ed.), *Trade, Development, Cooperation – What Future for Africa?* 2005, 44 pp, ISBN 91-7106-544-X, SEK 90,-

30. Kaniye S.A. Ebeku, *The Succession of Faure Gnassingbe to the Togolese Presidency – An International Law Perspective.* 2005, 32 pp, ISBN 91-7106-554-7, SEK 90,-

31. Jeffrey V. Lazarus, Catrine Christiansen, Lise Rosendal Østergaard, Lisa Ann Richey, *Models for Life – Advancing antiretroviral therapy in sub-Saharan Africa.* 2005, 33 pp, ISBN 91-7106-556-3, SEK 90,-

32. Charles Manga Fombad and Zein Kebonang, *AU, NEPAD and the APRM – Democratisation Efforts Explored.* Edited by Henning Melber. 2006, 56 pp, ISBN 91-7106-569-5, SEK 90,-

33. Pedro Pinto Leite, Claes Olsson, Magnus Schöldtz, Toby Shelley, Pål Wrange, Hans Corell and Karin Scheele, *The Western Sahara Conflict – The Role of Natural Resources in Decolonization.* Edited by Claes Olsson. 2006, 32 pp, ISBN 91-7106-571-7, SEK 90,-

34. Jassey, Katja and Stella Nyanzi, *How to Be a "Proper" Woman in the Times of HIV and AIDS.* 2007, 35 pp, ISBN 91-7106-574-1, SEK 90,-

35. Lee, Margaret, Henning Melber, Sanusha Naidu and Ian Taylor, *China in Africa.* Compiled by Henning Melber. 2007, 47 pp, ISBN 978-91-7106-589-6, SEK 90,-

36. Nathaniel King, *Conflict as Integration. Youth Aspiration to Personhood in the Teleology of Sierra Leone's 'Senseless War'.* 2007, 32 pp, ISBN 978-91-7106-604-6, SEK 90,-

37. Aderanti Adepoju, *Migration in sub-Saharan Africa.* 2008. 70 pp, ISBN 978-91-7106-620-6, SEK 110,-

38. Bo Malmberg, *Demography and the development potential of sub-Saharan Africa.* 2008, 39 pp, 978-91-7106-621-3

39. Johan Holmberg, *Natural resources in sub-Saharan Africa: Assets and vulnerabilities.* 2008, 52 pp, 978-91-7106-624-4

40. Arne Bigsten and Dick Durevall, *The African economy and its role in the world economy.* 2008, 66 pp, 978-91-7106-625-1

41. Fantu Cheru, *Africa's development in the 21st century: Reshaping the research agenda.* 2008, 47 pp, 978-91-7106-628-2

42. Dan Kuwali, Persuasive Prevention. *Towards a Principle for Implementing Article 4(h) and R2P by the African Union.* 2009. 70 pp. ISBN 978-91-7106-650-3

43. Daniel Volman, *China, India, Russia and the United States. The Scramble for African Oil and the Militarization of the Continent.* 2009. 24 pp. ISBN 978-91-7106-658-9

44. Mats Hårsmar, *Understanding Poverty in Africa? A Navigation through Disputed Concepts, Data and Terrains.* 2010. 54 pp. ISBN 978-91-7106-668-8

45. Sam Maghimbi, Razack B. Lokina and Mathew A. Senga, *The Agrarian Question in Tanzania? A State of the Art Paper.* 2011. 67 pp. ISBN 978-91-7106-684-8

46. William Minter, *African Migration, Global Inequalities, and Human Rights. Connecting the Dots.* 2011. 95 pp. ISBN 978-91-7106-692-3

47. Musa Abutudu and Dauda Garuba, *Natural Resource Governance and Eiti Implementation in Nigeria.* 2011. 74 pp. ISBN 978-91-7106-708-1

48. Ilda Lindell, *Transnational Activism Networks and Gendered Gatekeeping. Negotiating Gender in an African Association of Informal Workers.*
2011. 44 pp. ISBN 978-91-7106-712-8

49. Terje Oestigaard, *Water Scarcity and Food Security along the Nile. Politics population increase and climate change.*
2012. 92 pp. ISBN 978-91-7106-722-7